BLUNDER

*Breeding Bin Ladens: America, Islam,
and the Future of Europe*

*What Hitler Knew: The Battle for Information
in Nazi Foreign Policy*

BLUNDER

WHY SMART PEOPLE
MAKE BAD DECISIONS

Zachary Shore

BLOOMSBURY

New York   Berlin   London

Published by Bloomsbury USA, New York

All papers used by Bloomsbury USA are natural, recyclable products made
from wood grown in well-managed forests. The manufacturing processes
conform to the environmental regulations of the country of origin.

LIBRARY OF CONGRESS CATALOGING-IN-PUBLICATION DATA

Shore, Zachary.
Blunder : why smart people make bad decisions / by
Zachary Shore.—1st U.S. ed.
p. cm.
Includes bibliographical references.
ISBN-13: 978-1-59691-242-7 (hardcover)
ISBN-10: 1-59691-242-1 (hardcover)
1. Decision making.   2. Problem solving.   3. Intellect.   4. Stupidity.
5. Errors.   6. Cognitive therapy.   I. Title.

BF448.S45 2008
153.8'3—dc22
2008015233

First published by Bloomsbury USA in 2008
This paperback edition published in 2009

Paperback ISBN: 978-1-59691-643-2

1   3   5   7   9   10   8   6   4   2

Typeset by Westchester Book Group
Printed in the United States of America
by Quebecor World Fairfield

To the officers who study at
the Naval Postgraduate School

and in memory of
Gerald Feldman
an exceptional historian, mentor, and mensch
April 24, 1937, to October 31, 2007

CONTENTS

KEEPING CURRENT

B Y AGE THIRTY-FIVE, Thomas Alva Edison stood at the peak of his career. Presidents asked to meet him. Financiers hoped to fund him. Journalists vied to quote him, desperate to report his latest breakthroughs. Tourists crowded daily in his lab, just to watch him capture human voices on a disc and hear them back again. In a time before television, his image was so recognizable that a letter sent from North Carolina bearing only a sketch of his face easily reached him in New Jersey. The mere invoking of his name suggested genius, hard work, and the American "can-do" spirit. Then, in 1882, he illuminated part of New York City with his first central power station. So many other cities requested stations of their own that his company simply lost count. Edison had become a national icon, and the future looked full of fortune. There was a problem, however, one so obvious that Edison should easily have grasped it. The world was already outgrowing the very electric system he had helped devise. Edison's lightbulbs used direct current, but only alternating current could power both tiny lightbulbs and gigantic machines over vast distances. When one of Edison's star employees, a young man named Nikola Tesla, explained how they could harness alternating current and transform the way people live, Edison would have none of it. Edison had built his fame on direct current, and he could not imagine that anything more was needed. It was an exceptionally bad decision. By rejecting a new and far superior technology, Edison set the stage for Tesla to eclipse him.

If mad scientists had a prototype, Nikola Tesla would be it. Nearly everything he did had to be divisible by three. He would swim twenty-seven laps each morning. He would only eat breakfast with eighteen napkins set at his place. He would count the number of steps from his lodging to his office, and if that number was not divisible by three, he would circle around the block to make the calculation fit. Certain furry things repulsed him. The thought of touching someone's hair made him queasy. The presence of a peach produced a fever. In his later years, he developed an excessive, almost romantic attachment to pigeons. Despite these traits, or perhaps because of them, his close friends, like Mark Twain and Robert Underwood Johnson, found him utterly endearing.[1] For their friendship, Tesla now and then delighted them with his laboratory magic. The tall and boyishly exuberant Serb mesmerized his visitors by sending bolts of spectral light dancing across the room. He commanded electric fireballs to engulf his body and always emerged unscathed. Occasionally he literally shocked the onlookers by directing waves of colored currents through his guests. Mark Twain and friends were privy to a futuristic light show at a time when electricity was barely understood. But to bring his magic to the world, Tesla would have to confront the wrath of the man synonymous with electric light.

Tesla had an endless stream of ideas that led him toward inventions far before his time. He saw that the future was wireless and constructed the first rudimentary radio, even before Marconi.[2] Tesla built the first remote control device and demonstrated to amazed New Yorkers how he could use it to command a model submarine from a distance. He created the field of telegeodynamics, once even simulating an earthquake in New York City that shattered windows across town. His work inspired the cyclotron, a device used for smashing atoms that is central to subparticle physics. He made substantial, some believe decisive, contributions to the development of robotics, ballistics, and theoretical physics. When he died in 1943 at age eighty-six, the U.S. government confiscated part of his plans and equipment, believing that the military applications of his ideas could be immense. Thomas Edison clearly underestimated the talent he had in his employ.

After being rebuffed by Edison over AC power, Tesla was snapped up by an aggressive, farsighted entrepreneur. George Westinghouse purchased the rights to Tesla's patents and hired the young inventor as a consultant. Westinghouse then began promoting the use of AC generators, placing Tesla's system in direct competition with Edison's. Edison fought back with a protracted campaign to discredit AC by highlighting its many dangers.

One of his most egregious ploys involved a new form of execution. Edison convinced the New York State correctional authorities that death by electrocution in a specially wired apparatus would be fast and efficient. This so-called electric chair would of course require alternating current. Before Edison could release his device, it had to be tested. Neighbors began to notice that their pets were disappearing. Dogs, birds, cows, and horses were all made subjects in a gruesome experiment. When the day came at last for the first prisoner to be electrocuted, the procedure went horribly wrong. William Kemmler was essentially roasted in a spectacle too grisly to describe. Westinghouse, Tesla, and the many proponents of AC's tremendous benefits were outraged at this perverted use of their technology and vowed to strike back. The battle of the currents was on.

Despite Edison's best efforts to discredit it, AC was on its way to becoming the standard current for industrial production. Tesla's designs were simply too practical to be resisted, and Westinghouse grasped that the tide would eventually turn in their favor. The public just needed a clearer demonstration of the good that AC could do. That chance came with the arrival of the 1893 Chicago World's Fair. Edison and other electric companies hoped to profit financially by lighting that event. Westinghouse recognized it as a public relations bonanza. Thousands of spectators oohed and aahed as AC power illuminated the night sky in a light show that truly none had ever seen before. Electricity was still unknown to most people who used only gaslight and tallow candles. Thousands from Europe joined the crowds of Americans at that event. They came to see not just the dazzling colored lights but the star who made them shine. Dressed in coat and tails, the enigmatic Tesla put on a show of wizardry, to everyone's delight. Few in the crowd could grasp the scientific explanations, but all could marvel at the magical whirl of sparkling currents. Not long after their brilliant display at the World's Fair, Westinghouse telephoned Tesla in his laboratory with news. He had just landed the Niagara Falls contract. The power of those falls would spin gigantic turbines generating alternating current to run industrial machines. This was the company's most significant contract yet. Soon AC's tremendous potential would be undisputed. Tesla's dreams were coming true. So, too, were Edison's worst fears.

Edison was not a bad man. Although he could be stubborn and ruled by self-interest, he could also rise above pettiness when necessary. Once, when a fire destroyed Tesla's laboratory completely, Edison provided his rival with a temporary workspace in his own lab. Edison was a man who clearly saw the power of electricity and who championed a bona fide revolution in how the world would light its surroundings. In spite of that vision he could not accept that a modern world demanded more from electric power than what his system of direct current could produce. For all his brilliance, the man who invented the lightbulb was caught in a cognition trap—a rigid mind-set that undermined his own success. He failed to grasp a fundamental change occurring in the world around him.

Edison never recaptured the greatness of his early breakthroughs. Having lost the battle over AC, he poured nearly everything he had into a scheme to extract iron from ore by the use of magnets. After five years of tireless labor in the remote countryside, he had to abandon the effort. It was a total failure. Despite his gifted, inventive mind, Edison refused to adapt to changing times. Unable to accept that his phonograph had tremendous commercial value as an entertainment source, Edison insisted on its use as a Dictaphone and watched as another opportunity passed him by. In his eighties he enlisted Harvey Firestone and Henry Ford to back his search for a domestic rubber source. Again he failed. One employee even claimed that the inventor had secretly enriched his products with rubber extracted from condoms.

In a major corporate restructuring, the mighty J. P. Morgan, the banker who underwrote the Gilded Age, merged Thomas Edison's electric company with one of its rivals and renamed the new company General Electric. Despite the fact that Edison had personally electrified Morgan's mansion years before, the banker erased Edison's name from the company that would become one of the most profitable in American history. Decades after AC had become the standard current, the father of the phonograph kept repeating he was right. Edison's resistance to AC proved the biggest blunder of his life.[3]

Blunder is a book about judgment calls. It is the story of how smart people like Edison get caught in cognition traps and wind up defeating themselves. Most complex problems have complex causes, and no single factor can explain it all. This book offers one possible explanation for why people blunder. I suggest that we all sometimes fall into "cognition traps"—rigid ways of approaching and solving problems.[4] Cognition traps are inflexible mind-sets formed from faulty reasoning. They are the stolid ways in which people approach and solve problems based on preconceived notions and preset patterns of thought. Although cognition traps are forms of faulty thinking, each rigid mind-set I describe does contain a powerful emotional component. They affirm that our reason and emotions are so often intertwined. Yet as badly as our passions can muddle sober judgment, the stories of how people become caught in cognition traps do not, in fact, prove that blunders are inevitable. On the contrary, they strongly suggest that we can all make wiser decisions by cultivating empathy and imagination. As we travel through past and present examples, you'll see how true this is.

I believe that one key reason why we blunder involves the way we approach and solve problems. Without realizing it, we often fall into rigid mental frameworks. To understand how these mind-sets trap us, we need to know more about cognition—the conscious process of thinking. When most of us want to understand cognition, we typically turn to science. We expect the best insights to emerge from inside the well-ordered laboratory. While science can tell us much about reason and decision making, the scientist's methods of experimentation are only one way of understanding how we think. Another way is by examining our decisions as they actually occur in real life, rather than as they unfold within the confines of carefully controlled experiments. Fortunately, history has given us a wealth of cases for learning about how we think. This book is one historian's take on cognition.

Scholars from all manner of fields have been studying our thoughts to help explain the mental process. Neurologists, psychologists, cognitive scientists, even some social scientists—all are weighing in. But one profession has been needlessly silent. Historians have a unique role to play in these questions because they are ultimately concerned with how people think. Historians are not mere recorders of facts and dates. Although we care about what happened and when, our greater goal is to discover the causes of events. To do that, we need to know what thoughts led people to make history as they did.

When scientists study decision making, they create experiments in the present and watch as the future unfolds. Their subjects exist within a maze at least partly of the scientist's design, and they follow those subjects forward through time. Historians, in contrast, begin at the end. We start in the present and work our way to the past. After figuring out what people did, we then have to determine why they did it. We retrace their steps, exploring the labyrinth of options. Historians must also grapple with the challenge of getting inside our subjects' minds. Usually our subjects belonged to a vastly different culture from our own. The people we study typically spoke a different language, practiced different customs, and lived under completely different circumstances. Their actions are often mysterious, and the motives for their choices are opaque. Historians must act like detectives on a crime scene where the heroes, villains, and victims are all long gone. But unlike detectives, we are not just on the hunt for who done it; we must discover *why* they did it in the first place. To succeed as a historian, you must become acutely sensitive to how other people think. You must unearth the roots of other people's decisions, the good judgments as well as the bad.

Douglas Feith, assistant to the U.S. defense secretary Donald Rumsfeld, was one of the principal architects of America's war in Iraq. Feith believes passionately in learning from history; the rise and fall of the British Empire is one of his personal fascinations. His home in the Maryland suburbs contains an extensive library, holding some five thousand books, most of them works of history. Yet Feith accepts that history is no substitute for sound judgment. "There's a paradox I've never been able to work out," Feith admitted to Jeffrey Goldberg of the *New Yorker*. "It helps to be deeply knowledgeable about an area, to know the people, to know the language, to know the history, the culture, the literature, but it is not a guarantee that you will have the right strategy or policy as a matter of statecraft for dealing with that area. You see, the great experts in certain areas sometimes get it fundamentally wrong . . . Expertise is a very good thing, but it is not the same thing as sound judgment regarding strategy and policy."[5]

Politicians, policy analysts, intelligence experts, and scholars will be studying for years how America, possessed of the world's most powerful and expensive spy agency and scores of intelligent advisers, could have misread Iraq so badly. But the Iraq debacle raises much larger questions: Why do individuals, businesses, and nations, employing their best and brightest minds, and focusing their finest resources on a particular problem, sometimes go horribly wrong? With ample access to historical precedents, why don't people learn the lessons of history? I believe we often blunder not because our thinking is wrong, but because it is rigid.

To be clear, let me make a distinction between three important terms. A *mistake* is simply an error arising from incorrect
data, like believing that an electric wire is running direct current when it's actually on AC. A *blunder*, in contrast, is a solution
to a problem that makes matters worse than before you began,
like attempting to discredit a potentially liberating technology
rather than adapting to it. Finally, a *cognition trap* is the mental
framework that led you to a blunder, like the one I call static
cling, the refusal to accept that a fundamental change is under
way. This book is not simply a catalog of blunders. Instead, it's
a typology of judgment calls combined with the stories of how
they unfolded and how they were resolved. Each chapter defines
a different cognition trap and offers historical and contemporary examples of how those traps were sprung. Cognition traps
have nothing to do with a lack of intelligence. As you'll see
throughout these stories, they can flummox even the brightest
decision makers.

Blunder does not predict America's rise or fall. Instead, it explains the ways in which all nations, along with businesses and
individuals, weaken themselves. America's errors in Iraq, for example, will not destroy the nation, but they surely weaken it.
Most of the time, when countries blunder, they neither collapse
nor revolt; they just squander precious resources and set back
their progress toward prosperity, security, and strength. Eventually they regroup, right themselves, and blunder on.

Because I teach military officers at the Naval Postgraduate
School in Monterey, California, part of *Blunder*'s focus involves
international conflicts. My students come not just from the
navy, but the army, air force, and marines as well. And there are
many from other countries' militaries. One of the core courses
I teach explores the roots of war in the modern era. Through
historical study, we look deeply into the causes of war and the

conditions for a stable peace. One of the many lessons I hope my students take away is that thoughtful decision making can be cultivated and improved. The poor judgments made in war and peace often result from the same kinds of rigid mind-sets, or cognition traps, that affect people every day.

Blunder is not a book solely about nations and wars. It shows how the same cognition traps that ensnare policy makers catch us in other realms as well. Just as cognition traps sap a nation's strength, they can sabotage personal relationships and shatter corporate competitiveness. They foil our best-laid plans in nearly every arena, from international relations to romantic relations, from environmental management to health care to weight loss, and much, much more. Cognition traps are insidious, and once you finish this book, you will likely start spotting them all around you.

Throughout the stories in these pages you will meet a remarkable range of historical figures from antiquity to the present. All of them, in one way or another, have either fallen prey to crippling cognition traps or else skillfully avoided them. And some of them have done both. What they share is not any unique vulnerability to being unconsciously hoodwinked, nor any extraordinary intellectual gifts that helped them break the destructive mental habits that afflict us all. Nonetheless, they do share certain common features. My hope is that by the end of this book, you will have a deeper grasp of the characteristics that contributed to blunders and the traits that helped to avoid them.

Blunder aims to help us recognize the destructive mental patterns we all employ. But identifying the most prevalent cognition traps is not enough to overcome them. The second aim of *Blunder* is to suggest concrete ways for all of us to escape cognition traps once we find them. If we can spot those self-destructive thought patterns in time, then we have a genuine opportunity to break them. Naturally, it's always easy to look back at other people's errors and say how foolish they were. It's a much harder thing to be in the situation yourself and avoid the same mistakes. For that reason, in each chapter I contrast examples of people who blundered with people in comparable circumstances who managed to succeed. Even though no two situations can ever be exactly alike, we can still learn a lot from those who made sound decisions.

Blunder is a book about cognition, but it approaches the subject from a historian's point of view. Since historians love to tell stories, I illustrate cognition traps not solely with historical examples, but also by drawing on literature, poetry, and even a bit of clever folklore to ease us through the complex and crucial world of judgment calls.

Chapter 1

EXPOSURE ANXIETY

The Fear of Being Seen as Weak

POLICE OFFICERS ARE not typically trained to deal with elephants, and Eric Blair was no exception. But one morning in the mid-1920s, while serving the British Empire in lower Burma, Blair received an unusual call. Townspeople were reporting that a work elephant had broken free from its chains and was rampaging through the streets. Ill-equipped and somewhat uncertain, he gathered his rifle and set out. He soon encountered the trampled corpse of an Indian coolie splayed upon the road near a demolished hut. Blair prudently sent for a larger gun while he continued in pursuit. Once the Burmese saw him approaching with a weapon, they assumed he intended to shoot the beast, and they wanted to witness the show. Blair had no wish to kill the animal, especially after he spotted it grazing peacefully in a field, clearly no longer a danger to anyone. But the crowd, which had swelled to more than two thousand people, cheered him on. From their expressions and behavior, Blair understood that if he did not shoot, he would look a fool.

Taking his best guess at the location of the elephant's brain, Blair steadied himself and fired. The crowd erupted, but the beast did not fall. It only changed. It looked suddenly old and withered. He fired another shot. The elephant staggered but remained standing. Again he fired, and at last it fell, toppling with a massive crash that shook the earth. But still it refused to die. Its breaths were pained and rasping. The noise tormented him. Blair fired his remaining shots into its heart. Blood poured from the animal, but the tortured breaths continued. Unable to bear the elephant's suffering, Blair sent for his original, smaller rifle and emptied its contents into the elephant's throat, desperate to finish him off. The tiny bullets had no effect. Finally, not wanting to witness this any longer, Blair turned and left. He learned later that it took another half hour before the elephant died.

Blair was sickened by the things he regularly felt compelled to do and witness as part of the colonial police. His essay about the elephant was clearly meant as an allegory on imperialism. He wrote, "The wretched prisoners huddling in the stinking cages of the lock-ups, the grey, cowed faces of the long-term convicts, the scarred buttocks of the men who had been flogged with bamboos—all these oppressed me with an intolerable sense of guilt."[1] After returning to England, he resigned from the force and, against his family's wishes, determined to become a writer. Under the pen name George Orwell, he devoted his literary career to the themes of injustice and authoritarian rule. In "Shooting an Elephant," Orwell felt impelled by the Burmese mob, but it was not the crowd that incited him. Orwell was actually caught in a common cognition trap: exposure anxiety— the fear of being exposed as weak.

Exposure anxiety is more than just a fear. It is a belief that the failure to act in a manner perceived as firm will result in the weakening of one's position. In Orwell's case, he feared that by not killing the elephant, the Burmese would not respect his authority. Some Burmese might, in fact, have viewed him as weak for not shooting, but there were other options. Orwell could have devised a plan to contain the elephant until its owner, who knew how to handle the animal and who was a few hours away, returned. If the elephant had begun to act up again, he might have shot the elephant in the leg, wounding him to ensure he could not flee. He could have enlisted the aid of the two thousand Burmese spectators, using them to keep a constant vigil on the creature until new chains could be retrieved. It is entirely conceivable that a clever plan would have won greater respect from the Burmese. The tragic part of exposure anxiety is that it usually drives its victims to commit excessive force in order to appear extra tough. Orwell himself regretted his decision to kill, and some of his British peers saw it as a terrible waste, since an elephant in Burma served as a useful piece of machinery. Orwell's decision not only needlessly destroyed a valuable piece of equipment, it also reinforced in his own mind, and possibly in the minds of many Burmese, that he could be manipulated into actions against his better judgment simply by the fear of seeming weak.

Orwell experienced a highly personal form of exposure anxiety. He worried about his own image in the minds of those he ruled. But sometimes the victims of exposure anxiety project the fear of being seen as weak onto their entire nation. They worry that if their own nation does not act with unquestioned resolve, then other countries will not respect them. If this occurs, they fear that allies will desert them and enemies will be emboldened to attack. Instead of seeking creative plans that demonstrate moderation as well as resolve, they seize upon a simple, though counterproductive, solution: overkill. You might think that while exposure anxiety could affect individuals, it wouldn't affect whole nations. In fact, it has been a plague upon countries for a remarkably long time. Let's take a look at two examples. In the first case, in ancient Greece, exposure anxiety was narrowly avoided. In the second, it devastated part of the modern Middle East.

THE COUNSEL OF CLEON

In the year 427 B.C.E., a ship sailed from Athens on a grave assignment. The crew was bound for the Greek island of Mytilene, a region that had revolted against Athenian rule and lost. Worse still, it seemed that the Mytilenians had colluded with Athens's greatest rival, Sparta. Now that the rebellion was crushed, a warship was instructed to finish the job. The soldiers' orders were unequivocal: Kill every Mytilenian man; enslave every woman and child. Let no Mytilenian go free. But just after the ship was dispatched, some Athenians had a change of heart. What if such a harsh response was unwise? Should a faster ship be sent to overtake the first and prevent the mass slaughter? Two men stepped forward to advise their countrymen on the proper course. Each held diametrically opposing views.

"It is a general rule of human nature that people despise those who treat them well and look up to those who make no concessions." These were the words of Cleon, son of Cleaenetus, as he urged the Athenians to show no mercy to their defeated foes. "What we should have done long ago with the Mytilenians was to treat them in exactly the same way as all the rest; then they would never have grown so arrogant." Cleon objected even to the idea of debating the matter. "To feel pity, to be carried away by the pleasure of hearing a clever argument, to listen to the claims of decency are three things that are entirely against the interests of an imperial power."[2]

To show mercy is to show weakness, Cleon believed, and being perceived by others as weak would only invite further revolts and attacks. The perception of weakness, he contended, was tantamount to the loss of power. "Place yourselves in imagination at the moment when you first suffered and remember how then you would have given anything to have them in your power. Now pay them back for it, and do not grow soft just at this present moment, forgetting meanwhile the danger that hung over your heads then." Cleon's counsel was simple: punish them as cruelly as you can, and make an example of them to your other allies. Let everyone see that revolt will be punished by death. "Once they realize this," he insisted, "you will not have so often to neglect the war with your enemies because you are fighting with your own allies."[3]

Cleon believed that only a show of excessive strength would deter future revolts. Equally important, failure to respond with extreme force would, he was convinced, tempt future enemies to attack based on a perceived Athenian weakness. Like Orwell in Burma, Cleon suffered from the same cognition trap. Exposure anxiety typically leads its victims to overreact with excessive force, and the aftermath leaves them less secure than before the violence began.

If a vote had been called at the close of Cleon's speech, the Athenians might have been swayed. But then Diodotus, son of Eucrates, took the floor. Cleon had argued that there was no need to make speeches for any other point of view. He insisted that to consider opposing views was not just a waste of time, but bordering on disloyalty. Diodotus's first task therefore was to explain that wisdom cannot come through haste. "Haste and anger are, to my mind, the two greatest obstacles to wise counsel—haste, that usually goes with folly, anger, that is the mark of primitive and narrow minds. And anyone who maintains that words cannot be a guide to action must be either a fool or one with some personal interest at stake."[4]

Then Diodotus tackled Cleon's assertions head-on. Instead of pleading for mercy on behalf of innocent Mytilenians, Diodotus engaged in a daring act of rhetorical judo by demonstrating that mercy was in fact in Athens's national interest. "One of Cleon's chief points is that to inflict the death penalty will be useful to us in the future as a means for deterring other cities from revolt," Diodotus observed. "But if Cleon's method is adopted, can you not see that every city will not only make much more careful preparations for revolt, but will also hold out against siege to the very end, since to surrender early or late means just the same thing?"[5]

Diodotus was making a clever point. Murdering the Mytilenians would not serve as a deterrent unless all future rivals were identical to each other in the ferocity with which they fought. If those revolting city-states were in fact all the same, then Cleon must be right. Murdering all the Mytilenians would either deter the others or else Athens would have to kill them all in battle. But Diodotus believed that not all rebellious city-states were the same. Some were willing to fight to the death against Athens, but others might be persuaded, either by force or enticements, to resume their acceptance of Athenian rule. Some might even come in time to actively support it. Diodotus further believed that not even all the members within a rebellious city-state were the same. He pointed out that some of the Mytilenians had not rebelled, but had surrendered their arms to the Athenians. In some cases, he argued, a majority might even be persuaded to side again with Athens. Cleon's counsel saw no distinctions between city-states or the rebels within them. His policy of murdering all Mytilenians would create a perfect incentive for all future rebels to fight with unfailing ferocity to the bitter end. And why shouldn't they? Once they saw how all the Mytilenians had been killed, they would expect the same treatment. There would be no incentive to surrender. Just the contrary would be true: rebels would fight to the bitter end in the hope of avoiding certain death at Athenian hands. The Athenians began to realize what this meant. Future conflicts would almost certainly last longer and be more costly in both lives and treasure, for their enemies as well as themselves.

Nearly two and a half millennia later, on October 21, 2004, United States Army prosecutor Major Michael Holley rose to make his closing statement in the trial of Sergeant Ivan Frederick. The young sergeant had been court-martialed for his role in the abuses at the Abu Ghraib prison in Iraq. In words strikingly reminiscent of Diodotus's speech long before, Major Holley argued that excessive cruelty toward one's enemies is certain to harm the victor as much as the vanquished. "And I would remind you, sir, that the enemy fights on morale like we do, and this can form a rallying point for our enemies now and in the future. And I would also ask you to think about enemies who might surrender in the future. That's what we ideally want. We want them to be so intimidated by the combat power of the United States Army that they surrender. But if a prisoner—or an enemy, rather—believes that he will be humiliated and subjected to degrading treatment, why wouldn't he continue to fight until his last breath? And in fighting, might he not take the lives of soldiers, lives that might not otherwise be spent?"

Major Holley was arguing, just as Diodotus had done, that excessive force can easily backfire. It can make a person or a country less, rather than more, secure. Whether exposure anxiety drove the Abu Ghraib prison guards to commit abuse is difficult to say for sure. Having investigated the episode, the psychologist Phillip Zimbardo found that the guards themselves were asked to function under nerve-wracking conditions. They were fired on almost daily from neighboring buildings and faced attacks from detainees with smuggled weapons. All the while the guards lived in putrid, roach- and rat-infested cells with no sanitation, overflowing toilets, sporadic electricity, inadequate food supplies, and insufficient sleep. Under these circumstances, it would not be surprising if the guards had feared that the inmates would perceive them as weak. There were surely multiple factors driving their behavior, and exposure anxiety may have been only one of them. In the end, their excessive abuses not only sabotaged the guards' own careers; they also undermined American security.

In the war with Sparta, Cleon feared appearing weak. He, however, was not afraid for his own safety; he was afraid instead for the safety and position of his nation. Cleon had convinced himself that if Athens's enemies sensed any weakness, they would be encouraged to attack. This fear led him to overreact by advocating excessive force, the murder of every Mytilenian rebel. But Diodotus did not view all rebels as equivalent. He did not accept that the category of "rebel" contained members that were all the same. Where Cleon assumed that all rebels would respond the same to excessive force, something about Diodotus enabled him to see nuance within a category's members.

After Diodotus had finished speaking, the Athenians weighed the two opposing views. The vote was extremely close, but in the end Diodotus won. In the heat of battle the previous day, a ship had been sent to destroy Mytilene. Now a second, faster ship was dispatched to overtake the first before the orders to murder all Mytilenian men could be executed. On this occasion, exposure anxiety was checked by thoughtful debate, wise counsel, democratic means, and one other essential ingredient. The imagination to discern nuance within a category is what really made the difference.

Though millennia have passed since Cleon's time, cognition traps like exposure anxiety are still baiting us. Will we ever catch on?

MASSIVE RESPONSE

At nine A.M. on July 12, 2006, Israelis were arriving at work, beginning their day, when Hezbollah, the Lebanon-based movement that has been fighting Israel for decades, suddenly launched rockets into towns along the Israel-Lebanon border. The surprise attack caught Israeli forces completely off guard. But the rockets were a mere diversion. While troops rushed to the areas under fire, a separate Hezbollah ground force crossed the border into Israel near Zar'it, killing three Israeli soldiers, wounding two others, and seizing two more, Ehud Goldwasser and Eldad Regev. Attempting to rescue the hostages, Israeli troops pursued Hezbollah into Lebanon. The effort failed, and five more Israeli soldiers were killed.

Hezbollah continued its rocket attacks on Israeli towns, while Israel rained bombs upon Lebanon, killing an estimated 850 Lebanese, sending thousands fleeing into Syria and beyond, and destroying Lebanese infrastructure at tremendous cost.

On July 17, 2006, the new Israeli prime minister, Ehud Olmert, spoke to his nation and the world, delivering one of the most important addresses of his career. He needed to unify the nation behind his policy of massive retaliation. He had to find words that would resonate with millions of Israelis, sentiments that all could understand and share. More than this, Olmert, a less decorated soldier than the prime ministers who preceded him, stood especially vulnerable to exposure anxiety. He must have believed that he could not afford to seem soft.

"Israel did not seek these confrontations," Olmert declared. "On the contrary. We have done a lot to prevent them. We returned to the borders of the state of Israel, recognized by the entire international community." And then, the prime minister uttered the words that suggested a cognition trap was about to take hold. "There were those who misconstrued our desire for peace—for us and our neighbors—as a sign of frailty. Our enemies misinterpreted our willingness to exercise restraint as a sign of weakness."

Olmert believed, or claimed to believe, that Israel was now being attacked because its enemies perceived it as weak. Implicit in his remarks was the conviction that only a harsh and unmitigated response could secure his country's safety against a people who interpret peacefulness as weakness. By demolishing southern Lebanon, destroying its infrastructure and causing the deaths of hundreds of civilians, Olmert was taking the counsel of Cleon, that only the toughest response to attack can ensure security.

Ehud Olmert's use of excessive force, resulting in the deaths of innocent people, turned international public opinion against his cause. We may never know precisely all the consequences that followed from Israel's strikes into Lebanon, but one result is clear: Israel weakened itself.

At the war's close on August 10, when the United Nations brokered a cease-fire, Hezbollah remained intact, its standing in much of the Arab world was greatly enhanced, and the two captured Israeli soldiers—the original casus belli—were still not freed. (The soldiers' fate was not confirmed until July 2008, when Hezbollah returned their bodies to Israel.) Some 150 Israelis had been killed. The defense minister, Amir Peretz, was forced to resign, and the prime minister's approval ratings sank into the single digits. Roughly ten months later, the commission that Prime Minister Olmert had appointed to investigate the operation's failings announced its findings. A judge, two retired generals, and two academics on the panel determined that Israel would have been better served if the prime minister had considered other options besides the all-out military response. Olmert could have continued the existing policy of containing Hezbollah, the commission asserted, or he could have combined "political and diplomatic moves with military strikes below the 'escalation level.' "[6]

Given Hezbollah's ongoing, deadly rocket strikes, the commission's alternatives might not have sufficed. Sometimes diplomacy is no substitute for force. One other possible plan might have been to request an international peacekeeping force to be deployed within the cities Hezbollah targeted. If United Nations peacekeepers were being fired on by Hezbollah rockets, the international outcry would be swift and damning. Sympathy for Israel would have risen rapidly. Instead of acting unilaterally, the Israel Defense Forces could then have been joined by other nations in entering Lebanon to identify Hezbollah strongholds on the ground, possibly even with a part of the non-Hezbollah Lebanese government supporting the move. Lebanese public opinion might then have turned against Hezbollah for attacking UN peacekeepers and for incurring the wrath of the global community. Instead, Israel found that its strategy of excessive force left the country worse off than before its air strikes began.

Israelis have had several decades of experience dealing with attacks on their territory. Their statesmen and security forces have a long and intimate familiarity with Hezbollah. In light of all their historical knowledge, why is it still possible to miscalculate so badly? This is part of cognition traps' seductive skill. Though at other times we might know better, once they take hold of our mind-set, they lure us into false beliefs and imprudent judgment.

FOLLOW THE LEADER

We don't know enough about what makes people so susceptible to exposure anxiety, although one psychologist has studied an aspect of this cognition trap as it manifests itself in personal relationships. Dr. Matthew McKay, director of psychological services at San Francisco's renowned Haight Ashbury Clinic, has worked as a clinical psychologist for more than twenty-five years. In *The Commitment Dialogues*, McKay identifies certain fears that prevent people from forming long-term romantic commitments. One of these fears, which McKay calls "the shame factor," occurs in people who believe that others will not love them if they see them for who they truly are: normal flawed individuals. Dr. McKay describes it this way. "If our façade is penetrated, if someone catches a glimpse of us, we feel exposed, emotionally naked."[7]

McKay contends that shame produces tremendous ambivalence in personal relationships. He believes that some people live with a powerful sense of their own inadequacy. These people are perpetually trying to avoid feeling humiliated and to prevent others from recognizing what they feel is their true lack of worth.[8] According to McKay, this fear typically begins in childhood. The shame factor can be caused by parents who repeatedly belittled their children, instilling in them an "unworthiness schema." Another source can be what he calls "run-away moods," whereby people try to hide from others their bursts of emotion, such as rage, depression, or panic. To conceal their shame, McKay explains that most people create masks, personas of false selves. Typically they construct artificial personas to project an air of confidence, control, or flawlessness. When men suffer from exposure anxiety, they usually try to appear supremely confident. They are the know-it-alls who pontificate on everything and fear nothing. When women fear being exposed, they either act tough or present themselves as cool and quiet. Whatever the particular manifestation, the aim, McKay says, is "to keep the world from knowing about the pain and struggle inside."[9]

Exposure anxiety makes its victims worry that if others perceive them as weak or "soft," then their credibility will be undermined. From this follows a chain of fears. Their ability to get what they want will erode. They will receive diminishing respect. And eventually their status, position of authority, and aspirations for greater things will be stymied. In short, they fear a domino collapse of the things they hold dear. In reaction, they too often conclude that if they give in on a small point in which they may not have a significant stake, this will lead to their ultimate ruin. That is what can easily lead some to overcompensate, employing extreme measures to ensure that their position, or their nation's position, does not erode. Unfortunately, by overreacting with excessive force, they do not demonstrate their strength; they reveal their weakness. At the same time, they only diminish the position they had sought to protect. Contrary to what they would think, when someone admits to his or her faults, that person often gains the respect and trust of others.

Sometimes, of course, it's not only individuals who fear being exposed as flawed; it can happen to whole groups as well. An old Japanese legend tells how a man who was renowned for his impeccable manners once came to visit a remote village. Wanting to honor as well as observe him, the villagers prepared a banquet. As they sat to eat, all eyes were on their noble guest. As the mannered man held his chopsticks, everyone at the table tried to hold his own chopsticks the same way. As he meticulously removed pieces of fish from the main plate to place them upon his own, so, too, did everyone else. But then, by an unfortunate accident, as the mannered man raised a slippery sphere of tofu to his lips, he placed the tiniest bit of excess pressure on his chopsticks, propelling his tofu through the air and onto his neighbor's lap, where it landed with a terrific splat. After a brief moment of surprise, in order to preserve the myth of their guest's perfection and spare him any embarrassment, all the villagers at the banquet began flinging tofu into each other's laps.

The legend reminds us that people will sometimes go to extreme lengths to avoid being exposed as weak or flawed. But the interesting aspect of this story is that it was not just the honored guest who wanted to protect his reputation for perfection; it was everyone else as well. I think we often forget that it is not just hard for many people to admit their mistakes, it is sometimes even harder for those who support that person to accept them. This can be true for a parent in a family or the president of a country. When a leader refuses to admit an error, it may not be solely because he or she suffers from exposure anxiety, but because his or her supporters suffer from it as well. If their leader is wrong, the supporters sometimes feel that they must have been wrong for supporting him. To avoid that conclusion, they might prefer to cling to a myth of infallibility rather than experience the pain of correcting the mistake. And here is where exposure anxiety wreaks its greatest damage. Not wanting to admit an error, which they incorrectly interpret as weakness, they exacerbate the error by intensifying their original misstep. The counsel of Cleon tells them to keep killing, and kill even more. It says to show no mercy and make the punishments even harsher. It says never to change course or even listen to those who suggest a change. In military terms, they make the classic battlefield blunder of reinforcing failure, rather than reinforcing success.

What exposure anxiety victims never grasp is that admitting

errors and correcting them is not a sign of weakness; it is a clear sign of strength. It demonstrates that the person who erred is honest, responsible, and wise. That kind of leader, whether parent or president, is worthy of being followed.

BALANCING RESPONSE

Exposure anxiety is a perennial plague upon those in positions of strength, but it can be beaten without the appearance of weakness. The cognition trap's central dilemma is not that it encourages a strong response, but rather that it entices people to overcompensate by using excessive force when moderate force would be more effective. Striking that balance between diplomacy and force is one of the keys to prudent statecraft.

President Kennedy's inaugural address articulated the notion of a balanced response to threats. Delivered on January 20, 1961, the speech is best remembered for the euphonic phrase "Ask not what your country can do for you; ask what you can do for your country." But there is another section of this address, one less often cited yet far more insightful.

Set in the context of rising Cold War tensions, the president's words called for both national strength of arms and an openness to peace. It articulated a balancing of interests: conceding to exposure anxiety but tempering that fear with an overture to negotiation. "We dare not tempt them with weakness. For only when our arms are sufficient beyond doubt can we be certain beyond doubt that they will never be employed." Kennedy's wisdom came in acknowledging the necessity of preserving a strong defense while recognizing that superior force need not always be employed in order to be effective. And with classic JFK poetry, the president prescribed an antidote to exposure anxiety. "So let us begin anew—remembering on both sides that civility is not a sign of weakness, and sincerity is always subject to proof. Let us never negotiate out of fear, but let us never fear to negotiate."

These are not the kinds of words one often hears in contemporary American political pronouncements. They are words that reflect a particular worldview. I wanted to know what brought those words forth, so I contacted one of Kennedy's main speechwriters. Theodore Sorensen lives in New York. He is eighty years old and has just completed his memoirs. I wasn't sure if he would have anything to say about a few sentences he helped write nearly fifty years ago. After explaining why I was calling, I began to recite the sentence: ". . . civility is not a sign of weakness—"

"You don't have to finish the sentence," Sorensen interrupted with an almost audible grin. "I know exactly what you are referring to and I remember it well."

Sorensen explained what he had in mind at the time. According to him, a State Department policy in the 1950s instructed foreign service officers to get up and leave the room when a foreign country's representative challenged an American position. Sorensen felt that this behavior was counterproductive. He stills feels that Americans should talk with those who do not like U.S. policies. "When the current Iranian president, Mahmoud Ahmadinejad, sent that long letter to President Bush," Sorensen reminds me, "he never got a reply. I think it's simply an act of civility to send a letter back."

"What about this idea of fearing to appear weak? Why did you want to stress this?"

"This is one of the greatest problems in statecraft still to this day. All these Democrats today are trying to outdo each other for who can sound the toughest. They think they have to be militaristic in order to be strong. Kennedy was not a pacifist, but swagger and tough talk is not how you keep an alliance together."

"Why do you think Kennedy, you, and the others in the inner circle came to these views?"

"We were internationalists. We believed strongly in international cooperation, and Kennedy believed there was great value in world opinion."[10]

These were impressive views, but there was a problem. Although there were points in JFK's presidency when he escaped the temptation to use excessive force in response to exposure anxiety, his administration nevertheless committed an appalling blunder in the infamous Bay of Pigs incident, a botched invasion of Cuba in 1961. The Kennedy administration made other missteps as well. JFK's brief presidency shows how leaders can avoid a particular cognition trap on one occasion, yet fall right back into it on another. They can also avoid one kind of cognition trap while simultaneously being snared by multiple others.

The danger of cognition traps is that they come in many guises, and avoiding one is no guarantee of avoiding others. They crop up in every conceivable context. They ensnare us in all of our relationships, on the international, the organizational, and the interpersonal levels. Only an intimate familiarity with their hallmarks can help us to spot and avoid them. I want to explore some of those other common cognition traps. And to do this, I first need to introduce you to an entirely different and fictitious ancient people. Their blunder, and their story of cognition, begins with a prolific lamb, a burnt pig, and a startled little boy.

Chapter 2

CAUSEFUSION

Confusing the Causes of Complex Events

MISSING LINKS

IN A LAND far to the east, in the time when humans still ate their meat uncooked, a small boy made a marvelous discovery. Bo-bo's father, a swineherd, had traveled outside the village for the day, leaving his son with strict instructions not to play with fire. Bo-bo was a curious child, and all that day his curiosity swelled until it became unbearable. In Bo-bo's village, all the houses were built on stilts to keep them safe from flooding. That evening, when Bo-bo could resist no more, he made a tiny fire and accidentally set the stilts of his family home ablaze. Just then, his father's herd of frightened pigs rushed under the burning house for cover. As the stilts crumbled, the swine were charred alive when the burning house collapsed upon them. In stunned silence, Bo-bo waded through the smoldering wreckage of his home, found a burnt pig, and gingerly touched the carcass. Jerking back from the heat, Bo-bo thrust his burning fingers in his mouth and tasted for the first time the pleasure of roast pork.

The story might have ended there, but unfortunately for the villagers, the true manner of roasting pigs was not yet clearly understood. Bo-bo's discovery did not remain a secret. Word of Bo-bo's delicacy quickly spread throughout the village. Soon every family was setting its own house alight, searing its own swine herds, and relishing the treat.[1] Only several hours after the delirium from their feast had passed did the true cost of their meal become clear.

When the English essayist Charles Lamb penned this tale in the early 1800s, he had an obvious moral in mind. You don't have to burn down your house just to get roast pig. Metaphorically, Lamb wanted to stress how often people thoughtlessly sacrifice one thing they hold dear in order to get something else they desire. But without realizing it, Lamb was also pointing out a critical cognition trap.

Causation confusion—or *causefusion* for short—is any misunderstanding about the causes of complex events. Causefusion is a cognition trap that leads us to oversimplify, often at our peril. Causefusion comes in many forms. Sometimes we get confused about the causal links, meaning the chain of events that produce a particular outcome. In Bo-bo's case, the villagers thought that burning down their homes is what caused roast pork to appear, and in a sense they were right. What they missed was the full chain of events: first the house burns, then the pigs are roasted in the flames, and a tasty meal results. If they had recognized all the links in this causal chain, they would have seen that the burning of their homes was not a direct cause of their meal, but an indirect one, and one that could have been omitted if they had just built a separate fire for the pigs. Instead, they saw only a single cause, the burning house, as responsible for the cooked meat, and they acted on that belief.

Causefusion is, unfortunately, not limited to fiction. It is with us every day. But before exploring causefusion's destructive effects in the modern era, consider one real example from the ancient world. Imagine that the people in your town have been struck with a mysterious disease. They are feverish, vomiting, and weak. Nothing the doctors do can alleviate their pain. Many of them eventually succumb to the disease and die. Then you notice that all these victims share at least one thing in common. Shortly before the illness came on they had traveled close to the nearby swamp. The air in the swamp is heavy and thick. You conclude that your neighbors have suffered from that swamp's bad air, or in Italian, "*mala aria*." As the ancient Romans encountered malaria, they drained the swamps, and the incidence of the disease subsided. This correlation seemed reasonably to support the conclusion that malaria was caused by bad swamp air. Like the neighbors in Bo-bo's village, the Romans missed some of the links in the causal chain that produced the disease. Today we know, or think we know, that malaria is caused by blood parasites transmitted by anopheles mosquitoes who breed in stagnant waters such as those in swamps, where the air is also thick. If we still believed that draining swamps would cure malaria, we would not succeed in combating the disease, because the swamps are not the root of the problem; it's the parasites. And those parasites can exist in other places besides swamps. We would be expending a lot of time, energy, and resources on swamp draining, when the true sources of the problem lie elsewhere.

The Romans were not wrong to drain the swamps. They observed a correlation, acted on it, and the disease subsided, though it did not entirely disappear. Doctors, scientists, and all researchers can only work with the knowledge they have at a particular time. The blunder came much later. Because the swamp drainings decreased the incidence of malaria, the bad air theory went unchallenged. Rather than admitting that the true cause of this disease could not be determined for certain, generations of health care workers convinced themselves that bad air was to blame. Europeans clung to that incorrect belief for

more than a millennium. Only in 1854, when a cholera out-
break struck London, did an English doctor, John Snow, observe that the disease was waterborne, not airborne. But because
this contradicted the bad air theory, the implications of Snow's
observations were largely overlooked. That same year, Filippo
Pacini, an Italian anatomist, actually isolated the bacillus that
causes cholera, but again his discovery was ignored. It took another thirty years before the Prussian doctor Robert Koch re-
discovered the microorganism. At last the scientific community
was ready to consider that its previous assumptions had been
wrong.

No one should be blamed for not knowing the causes of
complex events or processes. On the other hand, everyone
should be held accountable for assuming certainty about causation when causation cannot be proved. Whenever we cannot
be sure about the root causes of events or processes, we have to
admit it and embrace uncertainty. Calling for the embrace of
uncertainty is not a glib aphorism. If we actually could keep an
open mind about causation, the implications would be profound. In the cases that follow, you will see how too much certainty has wrought blunders in our physical, mental, and societal
well-being. In some of these cases the true causes of events—
such as back pain, depression, and grief—are still unproven. Yet
the assumption of certainty could be undermining our hope
for cures, just as the bad air theory retarded our progress for far
too long.

MISSING LINKS IN THE FOOD CHAIN

The received wisdom about what kinds of foods are best for us
changes every decade or so, especially in the American diet.
Remember when margarine was thought to be the healthy

butter substitute? That fad lasted until margarine was shown to increase the risk of heart disease. These kinds of errors occur partly because of the same type of causefusion that befuddled Bo-bo's people. Those villagers missed important links in the chain of events that produce roast pork. Likewise, scientists have often missed key links in the complex chain that produces good health.

Michael Pollan, an expert on the history of nutrition, argues that food science is necessarily reductive because the entire food system, from the enzyme all the way up to the eater, is so complex that all nutrition researchers can do is break the system down into isolated parts and study them. The problem is that when nutrients are studied in isolation, we ignore the vastness of the system as a whole, making it extremely difficult if not impossible to know what any given nutrient's effect really is within the system. For example, the order in which we consume foods and drinks, or the combinations in which we consume them, can have tremendous influence on their benefit or harm. Most of us cannot absorb the iron in a steak if we drink a cup of coffee with it. That simple addition of a particular liquid into the steak meal yields a different nutritional result. In other words, if we want healthy meals, we have to understand the entire process of eating—with *all* of the factors that affect a healthy outcome.

Even when scientists are able to identify seemingly beneficial nutrients, they cannot always understand how those nutrients will operate in a real-life context, in the course of our daily meals. Fruits and vegetables are believed to help prevent cancer. Scientists have believed that it is the antioxidants in these foods that make the difference—compounds like beta carotene, lycopene, and vitamin E. Yet when these molecules were extracted from fruits and vegetables and made into supplements, they did not reduce cancer. The beta carotene supplement actually increased the risk of certain cancers. In other words, scientists were thoroughly causefused. They identified one element engaged in the process of nutrition without fully comprehending how the system as a whole truly functions. Nutritional scientists—pursuing the hot paradigm of isolating nutrients—failed to see the multitude of links in the causal chain that leads to good health.[2] The result was a classic blunder: a solution that made matters worse.

Nearly all scientists are constrained by the conventional thinking of the historical period in which they live. Only occasionally do exceptional thinkers challenge the fundamental assumptions of their times and bring about a paradigm shift. Although most of us will never revolutionize the fields in which we work, more of us could avoid the pitfalls of causefusion by embracing greater uncertainty about our basic assumptions. The aim of research in any field of human knowledge should not be to abandon the search for causation in favor of practical treatments. The aim should be to deepen our search for causes without falling prey to causefusion. Success comes partly by remembering that complex problems typically exist within complex chains of causation. Too much focus on a single cause, especially in the medical profession, can easily harm the people most in need of help.

THE DOUBLE BIND

As New Year's Eve 1999 approached, an emergency medical team burst through the front door of a twelfth-floor New York City apartment. Ashtrays strewn across the room were overflowing. The woman they confronted, the apartment's sole occupant, was flailing her hands uncontrollably in front of her own face. "Back off!" she demanded. "Who the hell do you think you are!" It was clear that she would not go peacefully. The approach of Y2K had unsettled many in the country, but the paramedics could see that something about this outburst was distinctly different.

Inside Pam Wagner's mind a cacophony of satanic voices was hounding her as it had been doing for years. She knew that the world was about to end, that she could not stop it, and that it was her fault for not having tried hard enough to warn others. She began to weep. She could not tell the paramedics how the voices, which had been silenced by medication, had returned to torment her. They criticized everything she did. They ordered her to do things she should not. In her own description of these experiences, she said, "I don't mention the National Security Agency, Defense Intelligence Agency, or the Interpol surveillance I've detected in my walls, or how intercepted conversations between these agencies have intruded into TV shows." When a paramedic extended a reassuring arm around her shoulder, Pam jerked back. "Don't touch me! Get out of my apartment!" she shrieked. She suspected that one of these men was connected to the five people who she thought monitored her movements wherever she went. Pam thought, "He has something to do with the other dimensions, the supermetal canister, and most important of all, grey wrinkled paper."[3]

Schizophrenia is one of the most debilitating and perplexing mental illnesses. It typically strikes young people in their late teens and early twenties. Without warning, the victim may experience hallucinations, hear voices, and lose the ability to distinguish the real from the imagined. Schizophrenics may become intensely paranoid and lose their capacity to think logically or speak coherently. In extreme cases they may become catatonic. Some 2.5 million Americans have been stricken with the disease, and for those observing a loved one who suffers from schizophrenia, the experience can be terrifying and intensely painful. Understandably, mental health practitioners have long been on a quest for the condition's root cause. That search, however, has been fraught with causefusion.

In 1956, the psychologist Gregory Bateson proposed a theory that he believed unlocked the mystery that had surrounded schizophrenia since it was first diagnosed. Focusing on the family dynamics within which schizophrenics functioned, Bateson discovered that the parents of schizophrenic children often gave their children conflicting messages. More often, Bateson found that the mother was the primary culprit. If, for example, she told her son that she loved him, she might immediately turn her head away from him in disgust. Bateson labeled these kinds of mixed messages "the double bind."

Bateson's theory immediately gained ground within the psychiatric community. His double bind theory enabled mental health workers to diagnose schizophrenics more readily by drawing attention to the family from which they came. It simultaneously provided mental health professionals with a guide for curing the illness. They would focus on the family.

Family therapy thus became the prescribed treatment for schizophrenics. There were just a few problems with this approach. The first was that although the family dynamics might improve, the schizophrenic children rarely showed any appreciable signs of improvement. Focusing on the family, therefore, did little to help the patients. The second problem emerged when researchers decided to study families without schizophrenic children. The results were surprising. It turned out, as you may have guessed, the non-schizophrenic families also gave their children mixed messages. In other words, there was a correlation between mixed messages and schizophrenia, but no demonstrable evidence of causation. As similar studies continued to corroborate the lack of causation, Bateson's once promising double bind theory fell out of fashion. In the epilogue of Pam Wagner's book, Pam's twin sister, Caroline, who became a psychiatrist, describes how common it was in the 1970s to blame families for causing schizophrenia in another family member. "By operating as though unproven (and eventually disproved) psychodynamic theories were fact, my profession caused untold pain to our family and surely many other families already torn apart by an illness no one really understands."

As Bateson's double bind theory was gradually abandoned, concentrating on a genetic cause for schizophrenia seemed essential. Psychologists began investigating the condition's occurrence among identical twins separated at birth. The assumption was that if both twins, raised by different parents, exhibited schizophrenic symptoms, then a genetic factor had to be at play. Sure enough, a significant percentage of such twins shared schizophrenic behavior, and today the hunt is largely on for a schizophrenic gene, or some other biological culprit.

There is a problem, however, with the search for genetic causes of schizophrenia. The fact that identical twins were separated already suggests that something in the family dynamic may have been amiss. Proponents of the family dynamics theory have been mounting a comeback. More recent studies have shown that after schizophrenic patients are returned to their families following hospitalization, those patients whose families express high degrees of emotion and robust criticism are more likely to suffer a relapse than those whose families do not involve this dynamic.[4] Other cases, however, reveal loving, supportive parents whose children nevertheless still suffer from this mental illness.

Where does all this seemingly contradictory evidence leave

us in the hunt for schizophrenia's ultimate cause? Was Bateson right that family dynamics bring on mental illness? Or do the twin studies and many other investigations reveal that genetics is the culprit? Scientists, psychologists, researchers, and families have been left in an awkward state of causefusion.

In the long search for schizophrenia's roots, causefusion has reigned partly because too many doctors have tended to focus predominantly on a single cause. Such a cause might exist, but by overemphasizing one factor at a time, like parental mixed messages or a particularly pernicious gene, the search has been slowed. And while most doctors and researchers might recognize that multiple factors are involved in the illness, the message delivered to patients and their families has not always made this complexity clear. In the process, patients and their families have sometimes suffered from the resulting treatments.

Most likely, the many ostensibly conflicting studies mean that family dynamics and genetic makeup are risk factors for schizophrenia, not necessarily the sole causes of the disease. Risk factors are those conditions that make something more likely, without necessarily causing them to occur. Sociologists sometimes speak of poverty as a risk factor for crime. There are many poor people who never commit crimes, yet the incidence of street crime is higher among the poor than the middle or upper class. So poverty can predispose some people to commit crimes when additional conditions exist. In the absence of poverty, some of those would-be criminals might remain on the straight and narrow. Under impoverished conditions, however, some people are at risk of committing crimes when other conditions arise. In this sense, heredity and family dynamics may both be risk factors for schizophrenia. Either or both may make it more likely that young people with a certain genetic makeup, or certain family dynamics, or both, will develop the illness. And if this is true, then trying to isolate a single root cause, or overemphasizing the role of just one cause, may result in serious harm to patients and their families. It will also limit our understanding of how the disease arises and how best to treat it.

If you find all of this causefusing, don't worry. Complex phenomena can leave even the best experts causefused. Precisely because the human mind and body are so complex, we often seek ways of reducing their problems, and even their functions, to simplistic models. In the early 1990s, the Harvard paleontologist and essayist Stephen Jay Gould wisely cautioned against causefusion. Writing in the wake of our newfound ability to map the human genome, he tried to dispel the idea that genetic makeup could explain everything. "We naturally favor, and tend to overextend, exciting novelties," Gould wrote, "in vain hope that they may supply general solutions or panaceas when such contributions really constitute more modest albeit vital pieces of a much more complex puzzle."[5] Gould understood that overemphasizing one cause over others can easily retard the race for discovery.

Each of the causefusion cases discussed so far has occurred when smart people overlooked important links in the causal chain. They focused too finely on one particular possible cause while ignoring many other factors engaged in the process. They focused on falling houses, not fire. They zeroed in on nutrients and overlooked whole eaters. They elevated single factors like family dynamics or genes without seeing the patients as enmeshed in a complex web of interactions, of which biology and sociology are each just a part. These cases represent one broad category of causefusion, the type we commit by missing key links in a process. But there is another broad category of causefusion, one that happens when we mistake the causal flow's direction. When this occurs, we can easily confuse cause with consequence by viewing causation backward.

The next time you're in the grocery store, peek into the shopping carts of people who are overweight. You might see that some are buying lots of diet foods: low-fat frozen dinners, diet sodas, or fat-free desserts. So if overweight people are eating mostly diet foods, would you conclude that diet foods make you fat? Probably not. More likely, the first thing you'd realize is that these two things, heaviness and diet foods, may be correlated, but that one does not cause the other. Diet foods might possibly contribute to the problem, but they are unlikely to be the true cause of the extra weight. The second thing you might realize is that we assume a certain direction in the causal flow. In other words, first x happens, and then y results. First you eat too much, then you gain weight, and then you start eating fat-free ice cream in hope of losing the weight. There's a natural causal flow, a direction in which causes and consequences follow one another. Sometimes, however, we assume a backward flow, that y causes x and not the other way around. When this form of causefusion occurs, we lose sight of the actual causes and focus instead on consequences.

KARP'S COMPLAINT

It usually swept over him without warning, leaving him with a dark sense of helplessness, alienation, or an indescribable emptiness. David Karp dealt with depression for decades. He tried everything he could think of to cure himself. At bottom, those treatments all fell into three main categories: psychotherapy, alternative healing, and prescription drugs. The first two categories of treatment made no meaningful difference to his pain. The drugs, in contrast, provided genuine relief, but only temporarily. Looking back on his first experience with antidepressants, Karp realized that in order to go forward with drug therapy, he had to accept the idea that the cause of his depression was biological. For a time, the drugs did work in lifting his depression, but invariably the pall of emptiness would descend again, and the drugs would be abandoned until a new concoction of medications could be found. Only years later did Karp come to believe that his depression did not, in fact, have a purely biological cause.

The story of schizophrenia treatment is in many ways parallel to the way American society has dealt with depression. The doctors who treat it, the pharmaceutical companies who develop drugs for it, and the countless therapists who diagnose it in the first place may all have fallen prey to causefusion. To unlock this cognition trap, and how David Karp came to his own understanding of depression, consider this.

Imagine that you have just looked down at your hand and noticed that your palm is bleeding. You reach for a cloth, a tissue, or anything to stanch the flow. You cleanse the wound with soap and water, apply a bandage, and fully expect the cut to heal on its own. But suppose a physician were to tell you that your wound has been caused by a chemical imbalance in your body. Would you believe it? This doctor can prove to you that vast numbers of microscopic white blood cells are gathering at the site of your cut, and he can demonstrate clearly that this change in your internal chemistry is not your body's normal state. The doctor tells you that your wound was caused by this chemical imbalance, and he prescribes some drugs that will return your body to its prior healthy state. Of course, there may be a few side effects, but nothing to be concerned about, he says.

If you are like most people, you will probably look at the physician with grave concern. You know that the cut was not caused by the chemical imbalance. It was caused, you suspect, by some sharp object you brushed against without noticing. The chemical imbalance, you tell the doctor, is not the cause, but the result of your wound. You know that the rush of white blood cells to the affected area is part of your body's natural healing process. The last thing you would want to do is inhibit that chemical imbalance.

In this specific case, the flow of causation seems simple and straightforward. First you are wounded, then your body responds to help you heal. Yet millions of Americans, and others around the world, are increasingly taking drugs to help them out of depression. Some of these people may have been convinced that the flow of causation in our minds runs exactly opposite to that in the rest of our bodies. There is a common perception that depression is caused by a chemical imbalance in the brain. This imbalance, some believe, prevents us from functioning normally. To return to a healthy state, they imbibe antidepressants. And these drugs appear to be highly effective at accomplishing their stated goal, most of the time.

But what if we have misread the causal flow? What if the chemical imbalance in the brain is not the cause but the consequence of our depression? What if a person first is wounded by some external experience, becomes depressed as a result, and the brain's chemistry then reflects the depressed state? This causal flow is just as plausible as the other, but its implications are profoundly different. In this conception of the causal flow, we have to ask what is causing the depression in the first place, and this sets us on a search for other, possibly nonbiological causes. From this perspective, the resulting depression and chemical imbalance in the brain may be part of the body's natural healing process. This would mean that depression, rather than something to be avoided, would be a necessary part of recovery. Given the stakes—the multi-billion-dollar antidepressant market, the known and unknown dangerous side effects, and the mental health of millions—it should be worth considering the possible nonbiological causes of depression. Fortunately, many psychologists recognize this case of causefusion.

In the magazine *Psychology Today*, columnists have tried to dispel the popular but unbalanced view that depression stems solely from a chemical imbalance. One columnist writes that biology and genetic predispositions may contribute to the illness, but psychological factors, such as a person's coping style and temperament, along with social factors like family dynamics and a support network, also play a role in the condition.[6] The evidence is mounting that our daily life experiences can affect our brain chemistry, not simply the other way around. Tests even show that psychotherapy—just talking about our problems—can alter brain chemistry as well.

Obviously, when people lapse into a severe state of depression, when they cannot get out of bed or function normally, drug therapies can be extremely helpful. No sensible person would suggest that drug therapies are never beneficial, and no one should argue that biology cannot be a factor in causing mental illness. The question I am asking here is whether depression is solely, or even primarily, caused by biology, as some suggest. This is the same question that David Karp confronted for years. Eventually he came to a new understanding of his illness.

David Karp was not just an average sufferer of depression; he was also a professor of sociology at Boston College. And as a trained sociologist, he had to contemplate, a bit belatedly, the many possible social causes of his condition. In fact, the father of his academic field, the French scholar Émile Durkheim, had made a landmark contribution to our understanding of suicide by arguing that modernizing societies were less capable of integrating their citizens into social networks. The effect of this social dislocation, Durkheim asserted, was increased depression and suicide. Influenced by Durkheim's and other sociologists' studies, Karp began developing his own theories about the causes of depression, based on interviews he conducted with other depression sufferers. Karp summarized his theory in an equation: medicalization + disconnection + postmodernization = personal dislocation.

Karp's first point is that many of America's widespread conditions—obesity, narcissistic personality disorder, etc.—have been medicalized. This is a mistake, Karp contends, especially regarding depression, because the body of evidence suggests that depression is caused by biological, psychological, and social factors. All are risk factors. Treating only one factor with drugs cannot truly cure the problem, and in fact it may even exacerbate it by preventing the depression sufferer from addressing all the root causes of his condition. Karp notes that many of the so-called diseases we believe have biological causes do not exist in other cultures, or they exist in vastly smaller numbers. Here are some of the contrasts he lists. The lack of joy—a symptom almost essential to diagnosing someone as depressed in America—is not considered a problem in Buddhist cultures. Many languages do not even have words for anxiety and depression. Narcissistic personality disorder, a condition increasingly diagnosed by American psychologists, is practically unknown in the rest of the world. Eating disorders such as anorexia and bulimia most commonly occur in capitalist economies. "In certain Asian societies 'semen loss' resulting from nocturnal discharge is viewed with great alarm and anguish because sperm contains 'qi' (vital energy), seen as absolutely necessary for health," Karp writes. He also points out that the frequency and severity of schizophrenia are much higher in societies with high degrees of technology. The more modern a society, the more prevalent schizophrenia becomes.

Karp's cases should not be taken to mean that all illnesses, or even the ones he mentions, have no biological causes. Instead, they should remind us that social factors influence the diagnosis—and therefore the type of treatment—of many conditions.[7] But they also suggest that social factors may be contributing to the causes of certain illnesses. Karp puts it this way: "The more pills we dispense for normal distress, the more we avoid tackling our most difficult social problems, potentially undermine personal responsibility, and perhaps even threaten the sort of diversity necessary for a flourishing democracy."[8]

Although human physiology is not identical to that of other mammals, one experiment with elephants might reveal something significant about biology and causation. From 1992 to 1997, a group of young male bull elephants went on a rampage. These elephants were orphaned and in musth, an elephant's natural stage of heightened sexual and aggressive behavior. What was unnatural was the killing spree. The young males murdered more than forty rhinoceroses in South Africa's Pilanesberg game reserve. During musth, testosterone levels are elevated, so it is tempting to think that increased testosterone, a biological condition, caused the elephants to rampage. But this behavior was excessive. Murdering rhinoceroses is not normal elephant behavior. The young males were out of control.[9]

Then researchers introduced six older male elephants into the group. The younger rampagers returned to normal. In fact, they quickly dropped out of their musth stage, which had continued for an abnormally long period. It was as if the older males said, "All right, boys, settle down and shape up. The adults are back in charge." Of course, we have no idea exactly what, if anything, the older males communicated to the younger ones, or why the presence of the older males had the impact it did.

Whatever the exact reasons for the younger males' change in behavior, the study suggests that external factors can play a critical role in an animal's internal biochemical processes. If that is true at least in this case, then the flow of causation looks like this: first an external factor (the loss or absence of older males) led to a biochemical reaction (the extended musth period), and excessive aggression resulted. If scientists had focused primarily on the elephants' biochemical imbalance as the cause of the elephants' behavior, those researchers would have missed an important link in the causal chain and would have overlooked at least one likely root cause. Again, humans may not be analogous to elephants in this way. The elephant study only suggests a possible window into how external factors can affect internal processes, and an overemphasis on any single cause risks mistaking the actual causal flow.

Elephants aside, causefusion has clearly affected the ways we understand and treat mental illness. At times families have been blamed for their children's conditions (as they were in Bateson's double bind theory of schizophrenia). At other times, biology was blamed, and the drugs used to treat the afflicted did more harm than good. In most of these cases, causefusion led mental health workers to focus exclusively or predominantly on a condition's single cause, and this tunnel vision prevented them from addressing the many other factors that might have been contributing to the problem. In *Eat, Pray, Love*, a beautiful, true story about her own struggle with depression, Elizabeth Gilbert urges that antidepressants be used only in combination with multiple measures so that more than just our biology is treated. "Medicating the symptom of any illness without exploring its root cause," Gilbert insists, "is just a classically hare-brained Western way to think that anyone could ever get truly better." Gilbert, who suffered from depression after a bitter and devastating divorce, decided to heal herself by spending a year eating her way through Italy, meditating in India, and apprenticing herself to a medicine man in Bali. Reflecting on her medication, she writes, "Those pills might have saved my life, but they did so only in conjunction with about twenty other efforts I was making simultaneously during that same period to rescue myself, and I hope to never have to take such drugs again."[10] As for Professor Karp, he, too, has succeeded in managing his depression better since he stopped relying solely on medication. He still struggles with the condition, but broadening his view of its causes has helped him incorporate nonmedical treatments and thereby keep the problem more in check.

All this raises a difficult question. What do we do when we just can't identify a problem's root causes? It's clear that we don't want to overemphasize the treatment of one possible cause at the expense of others, but patients need some form of treatment. We can't ask mental and physical health care providers to withhold their services until some future time when ultimate causation is at last established. The answer is that we need to be open to treatments that work, in whatever form they might come, even if we don't know why they work, and yes, even if we cannot prove that the treatment is actually causing the cure. John Snow and Filippo Pacini pointed out an alternative route to treating cholera, but because their observations challenged mainstream thinking, their insights were not pursued.

The mainstream Western approach to treating both mental and physical illness focuses primarily on specific biological causes. Consequently, medications and surgeries are the principal forms of care. Increasingly, however, more holistic, alternative approaches to illness are emerging, though they remain on the mainstream's outer fringe. These treatments try not to isolate a single variable within a complex process. Instead they explore the patient's entire experience with an illness: his biology, diet, family dynamics, emotions, and whatever else the patient himself believes might be a cause. In other words, they consider a range of internal and external possible causes. If these therapies genuinely make patients better, they should be incorporated into standard health care practices and covered by health insurance. The danger is that causefusion could lead some people to conclude that the factors these alternative methods are treating are themselves the sole causes of illness.

The best antidote to causefusion is an open mind. As we look at two alternative treatments—one for back pain and another for grief—try to embrace the uncertainty surrounding these conditions' true root causes.

Dr. Sarno's Divided Mind

Richard was not lifting anything heavy at the time. He wasn't bending over or torquing his back in any way. He was just walking down the street when it first happened. A violent pain ripped down the side of his leg. He collapsed in agony, clutching his leg and screaming. In the hospital, doctors ran a stream of tests to determine the cause of his pain. After CAT scans, MRIs, reflexivity tests, and more, doctors concluded that Richard had developed a spinal abnormality. Essentially, a bulge in his spine was pressing down on a nerve in his back. Only surgery, they told him, could relieve the pain and permit him to return to normal daily activity.

After months of recovery following the operation, Richard

found that the pain had not actually subsided. His suffering continued until a friend convinced him to see Dr. John Sarno of the New York University clinic. Sarno's unorthodox treatment has won him some small celebrity, including testimonials from the talk radio host Howard Stern and the TV journalist John Stossel.

Sarno contends that many back pain sufferers have had the cause of their pain misdiagnosed. He points to studies using a control group of men and women who do not suffer from back pain. When researchers compared the spines of these healthy individuals with the spines of back pain sufferers, the similarities were revealing. The group without back pain had just as many spinal abnormalities, bumps, lumps, and bulges as did the group with back pain. In fact, the healthy backs sometimes had bulges pressing against their nerves as well. These investigations strikingly paralleled those of the double bind theory of schizophrenia. Once someone took the time to compare those with a particular condition to those without it, the results strongly suggested only a correlation, not causation. Sarno therefore concluded that the back pain that his patients experience is not caused by pinched nerves due to slipped discs, bulges, or other abnormal spinal formations. Instead, he contends that their suffering has a very different cause.

Sarno's observations of patients' back pain mirrors some of the ideas suggested by Dr. Jerome Groopman. Groopman, who is both a physician and a writer for the *New Yorker*, suggests in his bestselling book *How Doctors Think* that one of today's great medical blunders may be a common form of back surgery. In 2006, doctors performed some 150,000 lower lumbar spinal fusion procedures, a process in which surgeons remove discs in a patient's lower spine and brace the vertebrae with metal rods and screws. Spinal fusion is a radical measure, yet there is no strong evidence to indicate that disc abnormalities necessarily cause back pain. Multiple studies show that many people have herniated discs, disc degeneration, and disc abnormalities, yet they have no back pain at all. One expert Groopman cites, Dr. Richard Deyo, the Kaiser Permanente Professor of Evidence-Based Medicine at Oregon Health and Science University, even argued in a paper that spinal fusion surgery has no scientific rationale and can cause more problems for patients than it solves. Nonetheless, surgeons continue to perform the procedure. There are, of course, financial incentives. Insurance companies provide much greater reimbursements for more invasive operations like spinal fusion than they do for an office visit in which the doctor recommends bed rest, ice, and aspirin, even though the more mundane prescription may be best. But Groopman does not believe that greed is the prime factor driving the procedure. Instead, he suggests that the larger flaw arises from an error in cognition. Surgeons misread the causal flow. They identify a disc abnormality and convince themselves that this must be the cause of the back pain.

Groopman's personal medical experience—his background not as a physician, but as a patient—made him exactly the right man to examine spinal fusion treatment. For several years Groopman suffered from an inflamed right wrist, which sent shooting pain up his arm when he typed, opened a jar, or performed other ordinary tasks. Three of the four experts he consulted gave inaccurate diagnoses, each jumping to conclusions about his wrist and scarcely listening to his story of how the wrist became damaged. At last Groopman found a thoughtful younger doctor who did something amazingly simple, yet exceptional. He suggested taking X-rays of not just Groopman's right wrist, the one that hurt, but his left one as well. And he took X-rays of the two wrists in gripping as well as resting positions.

Once they compared both wrists, the thoughtful doctor was able to surmise a possible cause. Because the bones in the healthy wrist moved differently during gripping motions, he suspected that Groopman had torn a ligament in the right wrist. The ligament tear could not appear on the X-ray; it had to be deduced by a comparison. Surgery restored that ligament, and Groopman recovered most of the use of his wrist.

How Doctors Think is really a book about causefusion. Nearly all the examples he cites involve physicians mistaking an ailment's true cause, sometimes resulting in the patient's death. Groopman uses the standard psychology literature to understand the various kinds of cognitive errors doctors make, and this is useful. But another way of thinking about the problem is to step outside that field's conventions. There may be many reasons why doctors and others misread the causal flow. One could be the failure to make meaningful comparisons. Why did it take four specialists before one of them thought of comparing Groopman's right wrist to his left? Why do spinal surgeons not compare, or not give weight to comparing, the backs of back pain sufferers with the backs of healthy people? Why have psychiatrists in the past so seldom compared depression victims in industrialized nations with those in nonindustrialized or non-Western cultures? After all, the very concept of a control group is part and parcel of modern scientific methods. And yet too often the experts ignore their basic training. Part of the answer must lie in the American profit-driven health care system, in which doctors limit the time they spend with any single patient in order to maximize the number they can treat per day. Even given these pressures, certain steps could never be taken— or omitted—without some plausible intellectual justification. If, for example, a patient presented symptoms of diabetes, most physicians would ask whether there was a history of diabetes in that person's family. It would be almost impossible to justify *not* asking this question. But it is perfectly possible not to make controlled comparisons when the doctor or the patients are causefused.

One characteristic that made Groopman's successful doctor different from the unsuccessful ones was his apparent degree of empathy. Groopman's thoughtful wrist specialist took a genuine interest in hearing his patient's story. He asked Groopman to tell him the full set of experiences surrounding the damaged wrist. The other experts Groopman saw scarcely asked for his input. One of the key messages in *How Doctors Think* is that those physicians who escaped causefusion exhibited empathy for their patients. They spent appropriate amounts of time with them. They asked probing questions. They listened to what their patients had to say. And once they did these things, their imaginations were activated. They then arrived at possible alternative solutions based on more sensible diagnoses of cause and effect.

John Sarno, too, is attempting to let his imagination break new ground, but here's where his ideas become more radical. After thirty years of examining patients with a vast range of physical pains in backs, legs, wrists, hands, and so on, he came to believe that the true cause of his patients' suffering stemmed from repressed rage. Sarno is quick to state that the pain his patients experience is not "just in their minds" but is very real. But he shows how, after all other known biological causes have been ruled out, those patients who still suffer pain are tender in areas of their back unconnected to regions where they possess any anatomical disorders. He even maintains that conditions such as stomach troubles, intractable rashes, and severe allergies, not to mention anxiety and depression, can often stem from repressed rage.

Having no training or background in psychology, Dr. Sarno constructed a theory that most people are burying anger produced by an unsatisfied id. The id, Freud's idea of the inner child, is the selfish part of us that wants to be taken care of and to have all its wants immediately gratified. Because we cannot exist within any social interactions without ignoring some of our wants, Sarno maintains that we develop resentments, frustrations, and anger. Yet we are unaware of this building rage, he claims. Only when we do gain greater awareness of it can we begin the process of healing.

Sarno can provide no evidence of causation—that repressed rage produces back pain or any of the other conditions he is treating. He can show, he claims, that many of his patients who have not had success with surgery or other traditional treatments experience pain relief by using his techniques for recognizing and reducing anger.[11] This, of course, proves only correlation, not causation. Yet as some patients deal with psychological issues of rage, their physical symptoms diminish. We cannot prove that one causes the other, only that they often occur in tandem.

Sarno's notions of mind-body disorders are not at all new. The literature on the impact of emotions on physical ailments is enormous. Deepak Chopra has attracted countless followers to his views of mind-body illnesses. Louise Hay is another of America's popular writers on the subject. Her well-known work *You Can Heal Your Life* has been a mainstay of the mind-body literature for years. In Britain, John Eaton has established a form of treatment he calls "reverse therapy," which, like Sarno's work, focuses on the role of repressed anger over caring too much for others' emotional needs at the expense of one's own. But probably the most intriguing Western treatment of mind-body illnesses has been developing in Germany. Its underlying

notions of causation challenge the traditional t'
the relationship between physical and mental health. .
tion is whether the mainstream or the alternative treatmen.
causefused.

Meet the Parents

For several decades, the German family therapist Bert Hellinger
has been practicing a very peculiar, yet allegedly effective, type
of group therapy. Hellinger maintains that traumatic events
within a family, such as the premature death of one member, often affect the health of those who remain. For example, if a
child dies from cancer, or a teenager from suicide, Hellinger believes that a surviving sibling may feel such subconscious guilt at
being alive that she herself becomes ill as a means of repentance.
Hellinger's years of work in family therapy have convinced him
that illnesses can become acute when the "natural" family order
is upset. He suggests that many illnesses stem from the unresolved emotional upheavals common in family dynamics.[12]

To help identify and then address the often murky feelings
family members can develop for each other, Hellinger created
what he calls a *Familienstellung*, or family constellation. The true
aim of his therapy is to demonstrate that family dynamics can
cause damage to our physical and emotional health. Here's how
it works. A group of approximately twenty people, none of
whom know each other, gather for an entire weekend of sessions. The basic setup is this: If it was your turn, you would ran-
domly choose people from the group to play the members of
your nuclear family, including someone to play yourself. Then
silently you would arrange them in the room as they stand in
relation to each other metaphorically. For example, if the parents were divorced and not on speaking terms, you might place

them in opposite corners facing away from each other. Or if the brother and sister were especially close, you might position them shoulder-to-shoulder. This process usually takes about five minutes, and then you sit down.

Next, the therapist leading the weekend session approaches each of these people and asks them in turn, "How does the mother feel here?" or "How does the little sister feel over here?" The players respond with whatever comes into their minds. After the therapist speaks with each player, he rearranges them in the room into a more comfortable order. He does this by continually asking each player how he or she feels in a new position. But rather than creating a tight-knit, one-big-happy-family constellation in a smiling circle, every arrangement turns out differently, often with certain family members at a distance and others unexpectedly coming together. This process could last anywhere from ten to thirty minutes. Only then does the therapy actually begin.

Once the players have been realigned, you stand up and take the place of the person who has been playing you. And you speak to the people playing your family members. But what do you say? And why would it be helpful to have total strangers act as stand-ins for our true family members? To find out, I partic-ipated in a Hellinger-style *Familienstellung* in Germany.

During my weekend session, a pair of sisters attended. In their presentation they showed that their father had sexually abused the older sister for years. This was not an uncovered, suppressed memory, but something the sisters had known about and dis-cussed before, yet their own relationship had always been strained, which was why they had come. In the course of their arrangements, and as they spoke to the man playing their father, it emerged that the younger sister had actually been intensely jealous of the attention their father had given to the older sister, even though she understood intellectually that he had been abusing her sister. The therapist made the younger sister confront the man playing her father and tell him how neglected she had felt. She also spoke to her actual sister and they discussed what had happened growing up, this time with the new knowledge of the younger sister's jealousy. Both understood the horror of sexual abuse, but neither had previously recognized the younger sister's feelings of neglect. This is what resulted from the physical representation of family members and the act of confronting them. It was not really role playing, because the players mainly kept silent. It was not their role to converse, but simply to be there. And in every presentation, a very odd thing occurred. The person whose session it was seemed to view the strangers in the presentation as their actual family members. At least, they came to speak to them with the same emotional intensity as if it were their actual father or mother standing before them. And every session without exception ended in tears, not only from the participants, but often from the onlookers as well.

This was true of another session, that of a woman who had come to deal with a very different health issue from the one that emerged in the course of the presentation. After she arranged her family, the therapist asked her about a large gap between the person playing herself and her sister. He asked if there were any other family members she had not presented. She said there were none. He asked again if she was certain. I was surprised by his persistence because it was not unusual for participants to put lots of space between themselves and others, but the therapist was following some strong intuition. After the second time, he asked, "Were there any tragedies in your family?" She said, "No," but then paused and said, "Well . . . I had a younger brother who committed suicide when he was seventeen, but that's so long ago it's not important."

An uncontrollable chuckle ran through the onlookers, not a mocking laugh, but one of embarrassment for her. It was so obvious to everyone else from the way she responded that the brother's suicide was in fact critically important. The therapist made her choose someone from the group to play that deceased brother, and you can imagine how the rest of it went. The problem was not only the guilt she adopted over his death, but the fact that the family had never spoken about it.

The therapist did not push Hellinger's views on the group, but all participants knew that behind the therapy lay the theory that many illnesses stem from unresolved feelings over family traumas. Part of what people found valuable in this therapy was the way it brought those issues to light in minutes, while traditional psychotherapy sometimes takes years to achieve this. Another useful part was the way it allowed for cathartic healing through the monologues that participants held with those playing their family members. But throughout the course of the weekend, something else, something much more surprising, was also occurring.

Something was happening not only to the people who were presenting their families, but also to the people playing the parts of family members. One woman, who was merely playing the part of the woman whose family was being presented, complained suddenly of a terrible tingling in her abdomen. The therapist asked if she could ignore it in order not to interrupt the session, and she said she would try. A few minutes later the player complained again. The pain in her belly had intensified. I could hear the trembling in her voice. I think that everyone in that room felt uneasy with her obvious discomfort. Finally she said she could not go on. The therapist then turned to the woman who had arranged the players and asked if she had ever had an abortion. There was silence in the room, and she said that she had. He asked her then to choose someone to play the aborted fetus. She then had to confront the fetus and say what she felt. There was nothing judgmental in it. The therapist had no antiabortion agenda. He simply asked her how she felt, and she said that for years she had been living with a deep sense of guilt.

Other members of the group began to recognize particular recurring patterns in the roles they were being asked to play. Several noticed as the sessions passed that they were being chosen to play the same type of role, like the unfaithful husband or the estranged brother. I thought this might be because the people selecting them had seen them in a previous role and in a sense had typecast them. But the therapist had another theory. One woman asked why she was repeatedly chosen as the family member farthest away from the rest, usually placed in the corner. At one point she had even been arranged in someone's family constellation outside of the room altogether. The therapist asked her if she had been depressed lately. She said yes. He asked if she had thoughts of suicide. There was silence, and then she nodded. In other words, these sessions appeared not just to be revealing things about the family dynamics of each presenter. The presenters seemed to be sensing things about the others in the group, tapping into other people's issues without consciously knowing anything about them.

Following each session, the therapist opened the floor to questions about what had just occurred. I asked how it could be that strangers could know anything about each other's most intimate feelings and family relations. He said that he didn't exactly know how, but he believed they could because he had seen these things demonstrated over and over again, like the woman who felt the pain in her abdomen. He said that some people believe that all living things, especially humans, are connected at a very deep level and in ways we do not understand. Women, he said, tend to be more intuitive and more closely attuned to the unexpressed emotions of others, even those they do not know. And oftentimes, he said, men and women pick up on the deepest desires of others without even realizing it.

Hellinger's curious form of group therapy raises many questions about causation. It suggests that powerful emotions can have profound effects on physical health. In a very real sense, he is suggesting that much of modern medical treatment is itself based on causefusion. He might say that while doctors prescribe pills to salve our emotional and physical ills, these treatments have managed to lose the true causes located in our family dynamics. Again, assuming certainty about causation can be dangerous. Family dynamics may be one risk factor among many. Nevertheless, if his methods help to heal, they ought to be explored. Just as the Romans drained the swamps and decreased the incidence of malaria, so we, too, should use the methods that work. What we should not do is assume we have located either the root causes or the wisest treatments until certainty is beyond reasonable doubt. A healthy skepticism about all causation is wisest for both traditional and alternative approaches.

If you're like me, you tend to be pretty wary of seemingly unscientific explanations. Sometimes the Hellingers and Sarnos of the world can sound not much better than ancient augurs. The augurs were the high priests of ancient Rome who interpreted the will of the gods by examining the flight patterns of birds. Depending on the birds' direction, number, type, and arrangement, augurs could purportedly both predict and explain the causes of events. Today we don't see any reason to believe that a link should exist between the flight patterns of birds and our individual fortunes. Any correlations between the two, we believe, are pure coincidence: correlations, not causes. But if we want to avoid the cognition trap of causefusion, it's worth thinking about what coincidence really means.

WHEN SINGULARITIES COLLIDE

Suppose you sneeze, and at the same moment a lightbulb in your room burns out. Would you think the two events are connected? Probably not. Why should they be connected? You sneeze from time to time, fairly often over the course of a year. And bulbs burn out fairly often. And in nearly all the times you sneeze, you don't see bulbs burning out, and vice versa. Imagine if the next time you sneezed, nothing happened. You wouldn't exclaim, "My God, a bulb didn't burn out! Just think of the odds!" Over the course of a lifetime, you will sneeze so many times, and so many bulbs will burn out in your presence, that eventually these two events are likely to coincide, maybe even several times. There's no reason to think they are connected.

The same would be true for those times when you're thinking of your spouse or another person you are close to, and suddenly he or she calls. Since you're probably often thinking of that person during the day without even always realizing it, and since that person may frequently call you over the course of your relationship, the two events are likely to coincide more than once, maybe even often.

But these coincidences involve recurrent events, things that are repeatedly happening and not out of the ordinary. But what about non-recurrent events, things singular in time, unusual occurrences? If one of these coincides with a recurrent event, it may not be so surprising. For example, a building collapsing. That doesn't happen every day or even very often. How many buildings have you ever seen collapse? The only ones I can think of are the twin towers on 9/11. Suppose my phone had rung at exactly the moment when the first plane struck the first tower. Would there be any reason to suspect a connection between my phone ringing and the tower exploding? It would not be surprising if a recurrent event like a phone ringing coincides with a singular event, because phones ring often. Aside from this, there's no reason to think there is a connection between the two—although that doesn't necessarily mean that there isn't one. There could be, but we can't think of what it would be or why there should be one.

But what happens when two singular events coincide? What does that mean and how can we explain it?

Imagine that you're standing on a street corner and suddenly you hear a remarkably loud sound. Just then you notice a set of crystal glasses shatter. Is there any connection between these two events? The answer may depend on which century and which society you live in.

Let's say you decide to investigate. You're curious, and you want to know what just happened. You soon discover that the sound was caused by the screech of a metal spinning wheel that had become misaligned and scraped against another piece of metal. You asked the shop owner if this happens often, and he tells you that he's been working with that machine for fifteen years and never heard it make that noise before. Now that he's whacked it back in line, he's back in business.

You and I know that the high-pitched sound probably caused the glasses to shatter. We suspect this because we know that sound waves can strike against glass, stress its structure, and cause it to break. So even though we have seen two singular events coincide, we have a plausible and even likely explanation to demonstrate their connection.

But suppose you witnessed this coincidence in early seventeenth-century America. If you told people that the sound shattered the glass, how do you think they'd react? In a best-case scenario, they would laugh you out of town. You would be an object of public ridicule. That night the pubs would be buzzing with the hilarious tale of your beliefs. "Hey, guys, get a load of this. This joker over here thinks that something called 'sound waves,' which no one can see, smell, or touch, travel magically through the air, pass through glass, and cause it to break!" You would probably be taken to the local asylum for the mentally deranged. And if you lived in seventeenth-century New England, you might just be burnt at the stake for being a witch, since you were probably the one who caused the glasses to shatter.

So here we have two singular events that coincide. Today we can identify a cause-and-effect relationship, but our predecessors a few centuries ago could not. More accurately, they may have come up with an explanation linking the two events, the piercing sound and the shattering glass, but it would have been a very different explanation from our own. Theirs may have involved witchcraft, divine intervention, or some other supernatural force. A tiny few might have withheld judgment, unable to offer a satisfying explanation.

This brings us to an obvious question. What causes can we not explain today that our descendants may explain with ease? Or here's a twist on the same idea. What explanations might our predecessors have had that we no longer accept, but that may in fact still be plausible? Is it possible that while the Enlightenment notions of scientific inquiry have brought us tremendous gains, they may also have limited our understanding in other ways? In our struggle to discern correlation from causation, do we discount plausible connections just for lack of demonstrable proof? Modernity has helped us take great leaps forward, but maybe we sometimes stumble in the Enlightenment's shadow.

I think it's fair to say that causefusion is common because our ability to identify true causes is easily impaired by our assumptions. We constantly make assumptions and are often not even aware we have made them. Here, again, our emotions cloud our reason. Arrogance could be driving some people to insist they know the cause. Exposure anxiety might be impelling others, such as doctors who fear they will not be respected if they do not speak with absolute certainty. People whose actions are guided by fear will always be prone to blunders. There is not much we can do to help them. As for the rest of us, we can do something concrete to protect ourselves from their poor judgment. We can question those authorities who insist they have the answers. We can subject their claims to careful reason, especially when we are not experts in their field. And we can stretch our minds to imagine alternative explanations, making our best efforts to disprove them. If we hope to avoid the cognition trap of causefusion, we need to train ourselves to keep our minds wide open, because the surest sign of a limited intellect is a closed mind.

The Sinatra Doctrine

More than two hundred border guards stared in disbelief. Their orders simply had to be mistaken. In direct defiance of instructions, they reinforced the iron gate. When the crowds swelled, the guards tried water cannons to disperse them. They had no effect. One young man clambered atop the gate, where hundreds had been shot trying to escape. Punching his fist in the air, he shouted, *"Freiheit!"* (Freedom!) as the mobs on both sides erupted in cheers.

Within hours of the official announcement, nearly a million Germans from East and West began dismantling the wall that had separated them for almost three decades. Some used pick-axes, others hammers, and some only their hands. It didn't matter what tools they used. That wall could not withstand the force of change. But what was it that really caused the Berlin Wall to fall? A surprising amount of causefusion still surrounds this pivotal event of the twentieth century.

Causefusion matters in both war and peace because the way we understand the causes of past wars affects the way we approach current and future conflicts. Policy makers and voters tend to adopt fixed explanations for how previous wars unfolded, and we apply the lessons we learned. If we believe that the Cold War ended because of a massive arms buildup, we may be susceptible to arguments for future massive military buildups to defeat a new foe. But if we understood that one did not cause the other, our political and military decisions could be wiser.

When Ronald Reagan died in 2004, television and radio broadcasts across America played that famous clip over and over: "Mr. Gorbachev, tear down this wall!" There stands Reagan on the western side of Berlin, the wall behind him. He tells the Soviet leader to take down the wall, and sure enough, the wall comes down, although a few years later and after Reagan is out of office. Thanks to that powerful sound bite, along with Reagan's advocacy of the Strategic Defense Initiative, or "Star Wars," program, many Americans believe that Reagan is largely responsible for the collapse of the Soviet Union and the death of communism. Americans have been encouraged in this view by the media and those who wish to link themselves to the Reagan legacy. The notion that Ronald Reagan was the prime driver of the Soviet Union's collapse may be one of our contemporary era's most striking cases of mass causefusion.

The argument goes that the Soviet empire collapsed because

Reagan's huge increases in defense spending forced the Soviets to try to keep pace in an arms race they could not win. As their economy faltered, economic and political reforms proved unavoidable. The stress of those reforms caused the hopelessly corrupt Soviet system to crack. There is, however, remarkably little evidence to support this causal chain of events.

It was hard not to like Ronald Reagan. You found yourself wishing for a grandfather just like him: strong and steady, witty and reassuring. He truly fit the role of president. It was perfect casting. Yet as much as we may have liked him, we can't in fairness credit him for things he did not really do. Many more important factors contributed to the Soviet Union's demise than the policies or person of Ronald Reagan.

First, the Soviet economy began to stagnate in the 1970s, long before Ronald Reagan's spending spree. Second, Soviet reforms did not begin until Gorbachev was appointed general secretary, several months into Reagan's second term. Even after Reagan announced his Star Wars project in 1983, it triggered no change in Soviet behavior until Gorbachev became general secretary. Third, the Gorbachev record reveals a man committed to a more Western European style of socialism than to the traditional Soviet style of communism. His reforms, both in domestic and foreign policy, were long in the making and not ideas he suddenly came to in response to the Reagan arms buildup. Gorbachev's radical policy toward Eastern Europe, nicknamed the "Sinatra Doctrine" because it permitted eastern bloc states to do it their way, meant that Moscow would not use force to control the Warsaw Pact. Once Hungarians and other Eastern Europeans discovered that Gorbachev would be true to his word, the Soviet bloc's breakup was unstoppable. Only tanks had held the east in place. Without the fear of reprisals, it was Eastern Europeans, and East Germans especially, who tore down that wall, but the man who made it possible by refusing to crush the revolutions with force was Mikhail Gorbachev. Boris Yeltsin, Pope John Paul II, and Soviet bloc leaders were all factors arguably more critical than Reagan. His personal diplomacy with Gorbachev, and the arms buildup he pursued, surely played an important role in easing east-west tensions, but Reagan cannot be credited with causing the death of communism.

Another aspect of causefusion comes in the belief that Reagan's hard line against the Soviets is what brought them to negotiate, reform, and eventually collapse. In fact, Cold War tensions abated not because Reagan was tough, but because he began with a hard line and then flip-flopped. Whatever his motives, Reagan reversed course over a short ten-week period from the end of 1983 to the start of 1984, adopting a new and strikingly conciliatory tone toward the Soviets. He reached out to Gorbachev, ceased speaking of an "evil empire," and launched a diplomatic offensive in stark contrast to the policies of his first term. Reagan did these things at a time when hard-liners inside the Kremlin were still in charge, still content to fight the Cold War. His prudent diplomacy, however, found a receptive ear once Gorbachev came to power. Reagan's success resulted not from tough talk, but from taking an initially strong stand and following it with a softer, gentler approach.[13]

The "tear down this wall" explanation for the Cold War's end is a widespread case of causefusion over the cause of peace. It credits an arms race with ending a war. Curiously, exactly the opposite claim was made about armaments regarding the First World War. Rather than a massive arms buildup being credited with producing the peace, on this occasion it was blamed for triggering the war. As Germany's naval expansion increased, the argument went, Britain felt threatened, an arms race followed, and this escalating tension propelled the continent inexorably toward war. Later research concluded that increased armaments had little to no effect on the conflict. Instead, many other factors were at work, including the specific war aims of Austria and Germany, as well as the more general clash between the idea of empire and the notion of nationalism.[14]

Another popular interpretation held that World War I happened by accident. Many believed that interlocking alliances and rigid mobilization plans made it impossible for statesmen to override their generals. This view was most famously advanced by the historian Barbara Tuchman in *The Guns of August*. Today it is clear that the World War I did not occur by accident, but instead because some governments chose war. And this tends to be true of nearly all wars, that they are not the result of chance, but the product of design. Causefusion over international conflicts can have dramatic consequences because correctly understanding the causes of past conflicts can be critical to avoiding future wars.

COMING TO CAUSE CLARITY

Causefusion—defined as *any misunderstanding about the causes of complex events*—comes in several forms. In one type we overlook important links in the causal chain of events. In another type we think that the consequence is really the cause. If there is a link between the different types of causefusion I've been describing, it is that each type leads to a sort of monocausal myopia. In all of these cases of causefusion, a complex process was at work. Sometimes the chain of events was misread or overlooked altogether, as with the "bad swamp air breeds malaria" belief or with the double bind theory of schizophrenia. Multiple factors were engaged in the process of contracting the disease, but only one was identified as the true culprit. At other times the causal flow was in doubt, as with the question of whether depression is caused by a chemical imbalance or the chemical imbalance is the result of the depression. Here again there was a tendency to isolate a single cause—in this case, brain chemistry—and to place it within a unidirectional causal flow. And sometimes causes have been advanced that were later found to have only minimal or no effect on the outcomes, as with the origins of World War I or the impact of armaments on the Cold War's end. In these examples, too, single causes were elevated above others and imbued with special status they did not deserve. Naturally, there are times when single causes exist, but complex phenomena typically have complex causes. Overemphasizing one cause, rather than exploring the many parts engaged in a process or examining the numerous possible risk factors for a behavior, is likely to produce solutions with consequences worse than the original problems themselves.

Fortunately, at least with depression, increasing numbers of mainstream medical practitioners are coming to rethink the prevailing views. Two experts, Jerome Wakefield and Allan Horowitz, have recently tackled the causefusion surrounding both the diagnosis and the treatment of depression. They challenge the dominant thinking inscribed in the standard reference guide for mental illness, the *Diagnostic and Statistical Manual of Mental Disorders (DSM)*, that intense sadness must be treated as an illness and medicated. They argue that "the conflation of normal sadness and depressive disorder in *DSM* criteria has handicapped biological research and created confusion that can potentially lead researchers to draw misleading conclusions from their data."[15] Horowitz and Wakefield have avoided causefusion by recognizing that blunders occur when we isolate one aspect of a complex process, viewing it apart from the process as a whole. "If brain researchers fail to consider the context in which sadness develops," they write, "they are in danger of misdiagnosing the normally sad as having depressive disorders."[16] When we learn to apply a more holistic approach to analyzing complex events, we will come much closer to sound prescriptions for all our physical, mental, and societal ills.

Chapter 3

FLATVIEW

Seeing the World in One Dimension

WHAT IF SQUARES could dream? Imagine a world of only two dimensions, a land where people exist as different geometric shapes. How would its inhabitants perceive the world? In 1884, Edwin A. Abbott, an obscure British high school math teacher, posed this question in a brief story, which over the past century has become a classic, remaining in print to the present day. In *Flatland* the concept of depth does not exist because its inhabitants are only shapes, and their society is organized, quite literally, along strict class lines. The more sides to each person's shape, the higher his status. The narrator, a square, is a schoolteacher. Triangles are the workmen. Women, who have the lowest social standing, are simply straight lines without any sides at all. The highest-ranking citizens of Flatland, who have evolved to have so many sides that they appear as circles, are the priests.

One evening, the hero of Abbott's story has a disturbing dream. The square finds himself caught in a primitive culture, a one-dimensional world called Lineland. The creatures of this world are nothing more than points traveling up and down a single line. The square feels deep pity for these pathetic point people, for they do not realize that there are actually two dimensions, length and breadth. But when the square attempts to demonstrate the concept of breadth to the Linelanders, they are incapable of seeing his sideways motion. The concept of "sideways" is so foreign to them that their minds cannot even comprehend what it could mean. As he moves to one side, he vanishes beyond the Linelanders' view, yet his voice can still be heard. Fearful of this heretical outsider, the king of Lineland orders his subjects to charge at the square and destroy him, which is when the narrator awakes from his nightmare.

Throughout the next day, the square tries to shake off the chilling scenes from the night before, but that evening, as he is preparing for bed, he has a vision. Suddenly a priest of Flatland appears in his bedroom. Never having been visited by one of Flatland's few holy circles, the square is honored, but confused. The visitor insists that he is not a circle at all, but a creature called a sphere. The sphere explains to the square that there is in fact a third dimension called depth, and he demonstrates this by moving upward. Naturally, the square is frightened and incredulous. He cannot comprehend what "upward" could mean. Like the Linelanders who could not perceive breadth, the square is incapable of seeing depth. Pitying the ignorant square, the sphere takes him by the hand and jerks him upward. Up they travel, through the square's roof and above the town, until the square is looking somewhere in the direction called down. Sickened by the foreign sensation and dizzy with disbelief, he looks downward to see his wife in her bed and the other townspeople going about their lives. Eventually, the shock of interdimensional travel fades, and the square makes a startling cognitive leap.

When the sphere returns the square to his bedroom, the two have one final exchange. Unlike the Linelanders who had resented and feared the knowledge of new dimensions, the square is grateful. He thanks the sphere for opening his eyes to a new perspective, and he wonders what the fourth, fifth, and sixth dimensions might be like. The sphere scoffs at the suggestion.

Trapped in his own flat view, the sphere cannot imagine any other dimensions beyond his own. But the square has grasped a priceless truth. He understands that the world is not as he had always viewed it. And if it could be different in one way, it could be different in many ways. Unfortunately for the square, his fellow Flatlanders cannot shake free from their flat world-views. Instead, they see the square as a dangerous lunatic and confine him to jail. Yet even from his prison cell, the square takes solace in his newfound understanding. His mind is now flexible and open to possibilities previously unimagined. In the truest sense, he has freed himself from the shackles of a flat worldview.

On one level the adventures that occur in Flatland can be read as an allegory on the British class system, but if Abbott's tale were merely an allegory, it would not have become such an enduring classic. Beyond its mockery of England's stifling class structure, Flatland is a clever warning against a confining cognition trap.

A flatview is any rigid perspective that constricts our imagination to just one dimension. It's thinking in a binary mode. We see people as either good or evil. We understand events as either positive or negative. We categorize others as either with us or against us. Since most complex problems typically contain shades of gray, the flatview trap limits our understanding of what we see, and therefore leads us to simplistic solutions. A flatview is an almost foolproof prescription for blunders. The tragedy of Mr. Abbott's tale is that although the hero manages to break free from the flatview cognition trap, his countrymen cannot expand their own imaginations enough to join him, and their own rigid mind-sets lead them to blunder.

Like the cases of causefusion surrounding the science of health and the politics of war, the flatview cognition trap is a type of reductionist thinking. And like causefusion, exposure anxiety, and all cognition traps, flatview stems in part from a lack of empathy and imagination. Although ignorance of a situation, a people, or history can hamper judgment, most of the time when governments, organizations, or individuals devote themselves to studying a problem, ignorance is not what causes blunders. Instead, it's the cognition traps like flatview that get in the way. Cognition traps occur for many reasons, but two frequent and interconnected causes are a lack of empathy and a limited imagination. Imagination permits us to perceive the world in multiple dimensions. It lets us speculate how life could be different for ourselves and for others. It enables us to consider values and behaviors at variance with our own without rejecting them out of hand. If imagination resides in the mind, empathy is imagination of the heart. Empathy lets us feel what others might be feeling. It empowers us to step inside another person's emotional body and experience his gut reactions. Too often policy makers overlook the critical factors of anger, resentment, and hate. Lost in the detached world of strategy and theory, they forget that their enemies and allies alike are ruled as much by emotion as by raw power calculations. In military parlance, superior force does win battles, but it rarely resolves the roots of wars.

THE OVERTHROW

Whenever Mohammed Mossadegh stepped before the Iranian parliament, no one could predict what theatrics would follow. His rants against the British sometimes involved uncontrollable bursts of tears. Often his arms would flail wildly in the air at the conjuring of some national indignation. Sometimes he would appear before the representatives wearing his bathrobe, and occasionally he would work himself into such a frenzy of patriotic fervor that he fainted dead away. With his long, droopy face, slumping shoulders, sad eyes, and pasty white skin, Mossadegh seemed at first glance to be the last man likely to lead a country. But his genuine depth of emotion for the Persian people, combined with his keen mind, administrative skills, and Western education, made him the perfect candidate to set Iran on a course for democracy. Unfortunately for Iran, it also set him on a collision course with the United States.

Mossadegh was unique among Iran's leaders. Aristocratic-born yet democratically inclined, he served as his country's prime minister from 1951 until his ouster in 1953. Before Mossadegh rose to power, Iran had been led by a series of rulers whose reigns did little to lift the Persian people out of poverty. Yet Iran was not a poor nation. It was blessed with one of the largest oil reserves in the world. The British-owned and operated Anglo-Iranian Oil Company, however, had been draining that oil and its handsome revenues away, selling it on world markets, and providing Britons with great wealth. Mossadegh believed that the resources of his nation should be owned and controlled by his nation, not by Britain. He passionately believed, like many leaders of developing countries in the 1950s and '60s, that his people had the right to enjoy the wealth from their own land. After lengthy talks with the British at last collapsed on March 15, 1951, Mossadegh and the Majlis (the Iranian parliament) voted to nationalize the Iranian oil industry. This act had nothing to do with communist ideology. It was nationalistic, and in most Iranian minds, it was perfectly fair.

Britain had a different view. Fearing the loss of considerable revenue and resenting the expropriation of its property (the machinery it had constructed in Iran for oil extraction), Britain imposed a blockade of Iranian oil exports by sending the

British navy to prevent Iranian tankers from exiting the Persian Gulf. The Iranian economy slumped as expected oil revenues evaporated. Mossadegh's popularity began to wane under the stress of economic hardship and unrealized promises.

Britain's stranglehold on Iran's economy merely served to soften up Mossadegh, allowing America to deliver the knock-out blow. With Mossadegh's popular support ebbing away, a thuggish mob gathered in Tehran's central streets demanding the Iranian leader's resignation. What most Persians did not know was that this was a mob for hire. Thanks to the CIA's skillful manipulation, prominent clerics and journalists had been condemning Mossadegh's actions for months, while profiting handsomely from the Agency's payroll.

President Eisenhower and his top advisers viewed Mossadegh's nationalization of the oil industry as a move toward communism. Nationalizing industries was something that accorded with communist principles. This was, after all, what Soviet Russia had done soon after the 1917 revolution. America also feared the growth of Soviet influence in Iran. Rather than recognizing that Mossadegh's decision was based not primarily on communist ideology but on nationalistic sentiment and a profound desire to uplift his people from poverty, President Eisenhower approved a CIA plan to oust the prime minister and replace him with the previously deposed shah, Mohammad Reza Pahlavi.

Operation Ajax was the CIA's first successful covert ousting of a foreign leader. Spearheaded by Kermit Roosevelt, grandson of President Theodore Roosevelt, the plan involved Roosevelt repeatedly smuggling himself into Tehran in the trunk of a car and persuading a key general in the Iranian military to stage the coup. Roosevelt also orchestrated the anti-Mossadegh street protests to increase pressure on the prime minister. The shah, who had fled to Italy, was provided with a plane to escort him back home once Mossadegh was seized. The CIA's success with Operation Ajax emboldened it to continue the practice in other countries, including Guatemala the following year.

Mossadegh was not anti-American, and compared to the clerics who have ruled Iran since its Islamic revolution in 1979, Mossadegh now looks downright reasonable. In fact, he could have seemed reasonable even at the time. Before the overthrow, Mossadegh had visited the United States and eloquently presented his case for nationalizing Iranian oil at the United Nations. He then traveled to Philadelphia to deliver a speech on democracy at the Liberty Bell. *Time* even chose him as "Man of the Year" in 1951. Given the choice of possible Persian leaders, the U.S. could surely have done worse. America's own choice, Shah Pahlavi, became renowned for his brutal repression.

As with nearly all historical events, the causes of Eisenhower's decision were multiple, but primary among them was the flatview that ensnared his top foreign policy advisers, the well-born Dulles brothers. John Foster Dulles, a Princeton graduate and practitioner of international law, had served as foreign policy adviser to Thomas E. Dewey, the Republican candidate for president in 1948. Although Dewey lost to Truman that year, Dulles remained active and outspoken on foreign policy and known for his aggressive stand against the global spread of communism. Much of Dulles's public persona was crafted for political ends. By appearing hawkish, he hoped both to intimidate the Soviets and appease domestic American opinion. His staunch anticommunist beliefs, however, were more than just bluster. After Eisenhower named him secretary of state in 1953, he pursued both overt and covert aggressive anticommunist policies. He remained in his post until shortly before his death in 1959. John Foster

Dulles's younger brother, Allen, served as director of the CIA from 1953 until 1961. Together, the Dulles brothers were influential in shaping Eisenhower's foreign policy. Their anticommunist worldview led them to interpret Mossadegh's actions as a tilt toward communism rather than the expression of national aspirations. The tragic result of their flatview was Operation Ajax.

Once restored to power in Tehran, the shah placed Mossadegh under house arrest for the remainder of his life.[1] The shah then embarked on a harsh reign during which he sharply curtailed his people's freedoms and did little to alleviate their poverty. As a consequence of the shah's increasingly brutal rule, popular support for a counterrevolution grew. The new revolution, however, was led by an extremist Islamic cleric, Ayatollah Khomeini, a man who saw America as the "Great Satan." When his supporters overthrew the shah in 1979, U.S. interests in the region and the cause of Middle East peace took a dramatic turn for the worse.

The hostage crisis that began in November 1979, in which scores of Americans were held prisoner for 444 days, symbolized the payback for America's ouster of Mossadegh years before. But the hostage crisis was only the beginning. To this day Iranian leaders have been hostile toward America, weakening America's ability to foster stability in the region.[2]

How different would world history be if America had not overthrown Mossadegh and installed a brutal dictator in Iran? Perhaps Mossadegh would have fostered democracy, and the Islamic revolution might not have succeeded or even occurred. We can only speculate on what might have been if Mossadegh had remained in power, but it is clear that America's support of the shah engendered deep resentment. This was the direct result of a flatview. Had Eisenhower, the Dulles brothers, and the other American decision makers been able to see beyond their Cold War prism, the Iranian people's tragedy, and America's losses, might have been avoided. In March of 2003, the former U.S. secretary of state, Madeleine Albright, expressed regret over Mossadegh's removal. "The Eisenhower administration believed its actions were justified for strategic reasons. But the coup was clearly a setback for Iran's political development and it is easy to see now why many Iranians continue to resent this intervention by America."

Because the flatview trap constricts our imagination and curtails our empathy, it often leads us to approach problems in a narrow, either/or mind-set. We simplify the world into those who are with us and those who are against us. And when we confront individuals who exhibit contradictory behaviors, actions that do not conform to our flatview, we don't know in which category to place them. Because flatviews do not allow for contradictions, complexity, or nuance, we interpret ostensibly inconsistent behavior as intentionally duplicitous, designed to trick us. Because of their flatview, the Dulles brothers could not accept that Mossadegh's moves to control his own nation's oil did not automatically place him in the communist camp. They could not imagine any other possible dimension in which Mossadegh could operate. He was either in the capitalist camp or with the enemy. There was no in between. The Dulles brothers may have had less rigid views on other occasions, but in this case the flatview cognition trap imprisoned their better judgment.

Just over a decade later, American statesmen faced a more complex character than Mossadegh, and they fell victim to the same flatview. This time the consequences for America were even more severe.

The Man with Many Names

He was intensely curious, eager for knowledge about the world beyond his home. As a young man, he journeyed out of his village and found his way to Boston, New York, London, and Paris. Later he lived in China, Hong Kong, and Russia. He learned English, French, Russian, and Chinese, studying key historical texts in their original languages. And he wrote almost as consistently as he read, although he never used his real name. His birth name was Nguyen That Thanh. Most communists in the period between the two world wars knew him as Nguyen Ai Quoc. While he used an estimated fifty pseudonyms over the course of his lifetime, the world came to know him as Ho Chi Minh.

One of the historic documents that impressed him most was the American Declaration of Independence. Ho was inspired by President Woodrow Wilson's call for national self-determination, enough that he petitioned President Wilson at the Paris peace conference following World War I. He assumed that President Wilson's pledges were not mere rhetoric. Vietnam was ready for independence from the French, and Ho hoped that the peace conference would grant his nation its freedom. The American president, however, was focused on Europe, and a little-known country in Southeast Asia did not warrant his attention. Wilson had more pressing matters on his mind. Ho's letters to President Wilson were ignored. Despite this rebuff, Ho's admiration for the sentiments enshrined in America's founding charter never wavered.

Flash forward twenty-five years. Ho has become the leader of Vietnamese resistance to the imperial Japanese invaders of his homeland. America and Vietnam now have a common enemy. Contact between Ho's fighters and the Americans was scarce, until a strange act of fate intervened. On a solo reconnaissance flight one day in November 1944, U.S. lieutenant Rudolph Shaw's engine abruptly failed. Forced to parachute into the mountainous terrain along the Sino-Vietnamese border, Shaw was picked up by a group of Vietminh fighters, the communist forces struggling to free Vietnam from French and Japanese rule. Shaw spoke no Vietnamese. None of the soldiers spoke any English, save for two words: "America?" "Roosevelt?" And with that simple exchange, Shaw and the soldiers marched for nearly a month over mountains and through the thicket of jungle that led to Ho Chi Minh. Shaw later recalled that when he heard Ho greet him with the words "How do you do, pilot? Where are you from?" Shaw was so relieved that he threw his arms around the Vietminh leader. It was a lucky break for Shaw, and it could have been an even luckier one for Ho. That chance encounter began a period of limited cooperation between Ho and the American Office of Strategic Services (OSS), forerunner to the CIA.

With support from the OSS, Vietminh forces exchanged intelligence with the Americans and conducted anti-Japanese activities. According to Ho's biographer William Duiker, Ho had hoped that although America was a capitalist land, Roosevelt would honor the Vietnamese struggle for freedom from French rule. He believed he could cash in his wartime cooperation with America for postwar support of his nationalist cause. For Ho and the Vietminh, it was a dalliance that would end in disappointment and ultimately in war.

In 1945, following the ejection of Japanese forces from his country, thousands of Vietnamese gathered in the western part of Hanoi to celebrate their victory and hear their new prime minister speak. Ho rose to announce his newly freed nation's constitution. Clad in a faded khaki suit and rubber sandals, the gaunt revolutionary declared, "All men are created equal. They are endowed by their creator with certain unalienable rights. Among these are life, liberty, and the pursuit of happiness." The battle against the Japanese was over. The war against the French, Ho knew, was about to begin. Perhaps his pronouncements were intended not solely for his countrymen gathered in Hanoi, but also for the few Americans in attendance. Among the onlookers were, he knew, members of the Office of Strategic Services. Once the Japanese had been defeated, however, Ho's assistance was no longer required.

Over the course of America's war in Vietnam from 1965 to 1975, the United States lost more than fifty-eight thousand troops. Vietnam lost more than three million Vietnamese lives, many of them innocent peasants. America spent billions of taxpayer dollars over ten years in an effort to prevent Vietnam from falling to communism—and ultimately lost.

Scholars and military experts have devoted enormous energy and innumerable pages to trying to learn the lessons of Vietnam. And yet there still remains no clear consensus beyond the view—on both the political Right and Left—that this war involved stupendous blunders. But exactly how this tragic error occurred remains the subject of passionate debate. The list of many causes must include the flatview toward Ho Chi Minh.

The debate inside Washington's policy circles cast Ho in simplistic, one-dimensional terms. Was he a nationalist patriot fighting for his people's freedom from foreign rule, or was he an avowed communist, wedded to the principles of international revolution? He could only be one or the other, most assumed. Because the flatview cognition trap stifled their imaginations, American statesmen could not perceive Ho as being both things simultaneously.

American statesmen suffered from the same flatview of the

war in general. They saw it in a single dimension, as part of a global Cold War struggle. Presidents Truman, Eisenhower, and Kennedy all provided support to anticommunist elements in Vietnam. Truman even did so covertly. He did this because he viewed the conflict as nearly all American statesmen viewed it— through the Cold War prism. Truman believed that France's support was essential to U.S. interests in Europe against the Soviet threat, and at the time, that might have been correct. To ensure French cooperation in Europe, Truman provided covert American military assistance to French forces in Vietnam. But once France's postwar stability became secure and its place within the capitalist camp was assured, that calculus no longer applied. By fiscal year 1953, Eisenhower's first year as president, America was covering 40 percent of French war costs, nearly half a billion dollars.[3] Most Americans never knew this occurred, but it was no secret to Ho and his supporters. American backing of anticommunist forces in Vietnam resulted not from domestic political calculations, but because the decision makers themselves perceived the Vietnamese struggle from a strict flatview.

Robert S. McNamara, America's secretary of defense from 1961 to 1968, presided over the Vietnam War's turning point when the United States stepped up its involvement, moving beyond mere military assistance to the South Vietnamese government to active military engagement with the North. In the gripping documentary *The Fog of War*, McNamara reflected on how the U.S. viewed the North Vietnamese actions. From Washington's perspective, McNamara explained, the North Vietnamese seemed part of a global Cold War that pitted communists against capitalists. The North was fighting, as Washington saw it, to spread communism's poison. In the zero-sum Cold War calculus, a communist victory in Vietnam was necessarily a capitalist loss. Vietnam thus represented more than just a remote, impoverished nation of peasants in Southeast Asia. Its loss meant more than just the loss of Southeast Asia. Vietnam represented one piece on the Cold War's global chessboard—a mere pawn perhaps, but whole wars can be won or lost by the capture of a single pawn.

In his memoirs, McNamara admitted that he and other key decision makers at the time misread the Vietnamese struggle. McNamara explained, "We also totally underestimated the nationalist aspect of Ho Chi Minh's movement. We saw him first as a Communist, and only second as a Vietnamese nationalist."[4] McNamara may be too generous to his colleagues. Based on U.S. actions, American statesmen seem to have viewed Ho in one dimension. All that appeared to matter was whether he was a capitalist or a communist, whether he was with us or against us.

In retrospect, it may be easier to see Ho's complexity, but the evidence was there at the time. The OSS had contact with him. American operatives had marched alongside him through the jungles of Vietnam. One American medic allegedly saved Ho's life when the leader contracted malaria. Ho had even met with General Claire Chennault, head of the famous Flying Tigers, the American-trained Chinese pilots who fought the Japanese by air. American statesmen possessed sufficient evidence of Ho's genuine nationalist intentions. But because he was also an avowed communist, it was extremely difficult for those statesmen to imagine how Ho could be both things at once. If they could have put themselves in Ho's position, they might have seen that both ideologies were a means to an end. Nationalism provided a means of mobilizing the population against outside invaders, ultimately freeing his country to become what he believed would be a more equitable society under communism. Likewise, communism offered a range of benefits to Vietnamese villagers, such as more even land distribution, fairer taxation, and greater social mobility for the poorer classes. By espousing these communist values, Ho could mobilize the populace to fight the foreigners and win his nation's freedom. To the American mind, communism and nationalism were largely mutually exclusive. To Ho's mind, they may have been perfectly compatible.

President Lyndon Johnson, McNamara, and the other key decision makers were imprisoned in an unimaginative flatview. It was the same type of thinking that led Eisenhower and the Dulles brothers to overthrow Mohammed Mossadegh. It was the same flatview that imprisoned Edwin Abbott's square, until the square broke free from the cognition trap with a little help from a sphere. Unfortunately, in real life, spheres seldom come to our aid. Instead, we can only guard against cognition traps by developing our empathy, exercising imagination, and rejecting reductionist solutions. All these things can be fostered by discerning nuance within categories.

A Jungle out There

On June 16, 1948, three British men were working on a rubber plantation in the British colony of Malaya. From out of the jungle, rebels of the Malayan Communist Party struck. In the surprise attack, all three Britons were murdered and the rebels fled. This was the first shot in what the British euphemistically dubbed the Malayan Emergency. The twelve-year guerrilla war pitted British army soldiers against Malayan (now Malaysian) terrorist attacks. It was a war the British eventually won, but they had to travel up a steep learning curve, and, along the way, circumvent cognition traps.

The Malayan Communist Party (MCP) drew its support mainly from the rural Chinese living on the outskirts of towns. Like Ho and the Vietminh, the MCP promised material advancement to villagers who felt blocked from upward mobility. At first, the MCP's message held much appeal, especially when compared with the alternative: a continuation of British rule at a time when nationalist aspirations were sweeping the postwar world. The age of empires was passing, and Malayans were beginning to demand the same type of independence as Indians, Africans, and other colonized peoples.

The British initially employed the same harsh imperial tactics against Malayans that they had used in some of their other colonies. From 1948 to 1952, the generals in charge of combating the insurgents pursued a policy of collective punishment. Lumping all Malayans together as potential rebels, the British imposed mass detention for those suspected of ties to communist terrorists (CT, as they came to be known). They left thousands of innocent young men virtual prisoners in makeshift interrogation centers. They routinely imposed strict curfews on entire localities deemed uncooperative, and they levied steep fines upon whole communities that did not overtly aid the anticommunist crusade. Mass roundups created headaches for the British as well. The camps drained manpower away from the hunt for insurgency leaders, and it failed to discriminate between actual communist terrorists, those merely sympathetic to communist values, those who were pro-British, and those who simply didn't care about the conflict and wanted to be left alone by all sides. One of the leading British commanders expressed remarkably crass views of the enemy, even by the standards of the day. He wrote to a colleague that the Chinese "as you know are notoriously inclined to lean toward whichever side frightens them more."[5] Attitudes like this both validated and furthered the British army's draconian measures. The result was what you might expect. MCP enrollment swelled. The enemy's strength increased.

In 1951, a new Conservative government was elected in England, and it fully intended to see Malaya become independent. The British refused, of course, to let what they saw as communist terrorists take over once Britain withdrew. The strategy of excessive, indiscriminate force was failing. The war was dragging on. In his most succinct, military manner, the famed World War II hero, Field Marshal Bernard Montgomery, wrote the British colonial secretary, Oliver Lyttelton, a note on the crisis as follows:

> Dear Lyttelton,
> Malaya
> We must have a plan.
> Secondly, we must have a man.
> When we have a plan and a man, we shall succeed: not otherwise.
> Yours Sincerely,
> Montgomery[6]

The man with the plan was General Gerald Templer. Templer had directed the British zone of occupied West Germany after World War II. His background in intelligence work combined with his administrative experience may have helped him to shift strategy in Malaya, but more crucially, his ability to avoid a flatview made the difference. Templer quickly undertook a wholly new campaign to determine what motivated the rural Chinese. He wanted to understand what was driving the insurgency and why rural Chinese would follow Chin Peng, the MCP's elusive leader.

Templer's first task, as in most counterinsurgency campaigns, was to ensure the noncombatant population's security. Without Chinese confidence in British soldiers, the Chinese would not supply the vital intelligence necessary for breaking MCP cells. Local intelligence is always crucial in defeating any insurgency. Similarly, Templer understood that the Chinese Malayans would not march in the anticommunist rallies if they thought the British could not protect them. But more than this, he recognized that not all CT were hardened, dogmatic true believers. Some of them, he knew, had to be young men caught up in the struggle for many other reasons than genuine ideological conviction. If British army tactics were purely punitive and excessively cruel, then no CT would ever surrender to British units when cornered. And why should they? Just as with the Mytilenians of ancient Greece, the Malayan Chinese made the same calculation. It was better to fight to the death if the alternative is indiscriminate punishment by the foreigner. Templer, like Diodotus, discerned the differences among local Chinese. He ordered all previous excessively harsh tactics against innocent villagers to cease.

Because Templer did not view all CT alike, he increased the use of surrendered enemy personnel (SEP) in both active combat operations in the jungle and psychological operations in the air. He used voice aircraft missions, planes that broadcast spoken messages, to fly over jungle regions where CT were active. Former CT broadcast messages about why they had surrendered and switched sides. Learning that women in CT areas were giving birth under extremely unsafe conditions, the British produced remarkably effective pamphlets showing Chinese women in clean, modern maternity clinics inside the British zones. These tactics and many other psychological operations sapped support away from the CT.

Templer further learned that providing security was not enough. It was also necessary to match what Peng promised and surpass it. Templer forcibly resettled many rural Chinese into new villages, far from the MCP jungle strongholds. At first, many villagers resented the relocation, but Templer ensured that "aftercare" would more than compensate them. The British provided new economic opportunities in addition to health care, educational facilities, and more modern amenities. In time, Britain was able to show convincingly that it, and not Peng, could provide the material benefits most attractive to rural Chinese.

Eventually Peng and his dwindling band of insurgents sued for peace, and Peng himself fled to China, where he still lives. The historian Ian Ward tracked him down and persuaded him to recount the war as he saw it. Looking back some fifty-five years since the start of his uprising, Peng declared that while he still believes in the equitable redistribution of wealth, he had abandoned the idea of a dictatorship of the proletariat. Assessing the reasons for his failure in what is now Malaysia, Peng placed the blame on British propaganda. "It was my choice to lead from the shadows, away from the limelight," he wrote in 2003. "This was my undoing. My elusive approach to the struggle made it easier for British propaganda to mould the image they wanted for the MCP Secretary General—brutal, ruthless, bloodthirsty and indifferent to suffering."[7]

British forces had to learn from their initial errors in Malaya and adopt a new strategy based on winning the confidence of Peng's supporters. Part of what enabled their success was a change in mental habit. Kumar Ramakrishna, a scholar who has studied the role of propaganda in Britain's experience, observed, "The problem was that British administrators and soldiers took years to jettison certain habits of mind that had been forged during the long experience of Imperial policing." They had a propensity to stereotype a particular ethnic group as "cunning and in need of a firm hand to keep them in check."[8] Templer and his staff were essential in fostering a new worldview throughout the British military organization in Malaya. They trained their military to see the insurgents as people first. Many of Peng's backers, after all, were not guerrillas but peasants, people struggling to survive each day under difficult conditions. They knew little of Soviet geopolitics and cared even less. What they wanted was security and material advancement, and Templer helped provide both. After their initial blunders, the British military relearned an old lesson, that the local population, not the force of arms, is the true center of gravity (the source of power) in any insurgency.

Another of Britain's advantages was its ability to perceive each country as its own unique entity. As a result, the British Army did not attempt to impose a universal, rigid doctrine upon its own forces. Instead, the army understood that military doctrine alone could not win the war. A combined political-military approach was necessary. The British needed the support of the local population in order to defeat the indigenous communists, and that support could come only after they discerned how this insurgency differed from prior ones. This was a critical lesson, one that the American army in Vietnam never fully mastered.[9]

So if Templer and his army could escape the flatview trap in Malaya, why did McNamara and his colleagues get caught by a flatview of Ho and Vietnam? Part of the American defense secretary's explanation for this error was the lack of knowledgeable Far East and Southeast Asian experts in government. The three most knowledgeable experts had been purged during the McCarthy trials of the 1950s. "Without men like these to provide sophisticated insights," McNamara declared, "we, certainly I, badly misread China's objectives and mistook its bellicose rhetoric to imply a drive for regional hegemony."[10] He called the foundations of his own coterie's decision making "gravely flawed."[11]

More Vietnam experts might not have hurt, but they were not the most critical missing ingredient. Remember Douglas Feith, the defense department undersecretary I cited in the introduction? He had told the *New Yorker* reporter about judgment. He said that "the great experts in certain areas sometimes get it fundamentally wrong . . . Expertise is a very good thing, but it is not the same thing as *sound judgment* regarding strategy and policy"[12]

I think Doug Feith is correct. Expertise is not a guarantee of sound judgment. If the area experts lack the imagination to look beyond a single dimension, no amount of expertise will produce wise policies. The Washington decision makers themselves needed to be aware of their flatviews. As McNamara admitted, they were not cognizant of the cognition traps into which they had fallen. Their reasoning went unchallenged.

General Templer, conversely, recognized that harsh tactics stemmed from a flatview inappropriate to the Malayan case. He also saw that Malaya's Chinese minority was fighting in part for equality, not for the spread of global communism. A flatview of their struggle shattered under close inspection. Perhaps without even realizing it, Templer had run a cognition trap check, and once the cognition minefield was cleared, his chances for success dramatically improved.

In contrast, Johnson, McNamara, and many others fell headlong into cognition traps over Vietnam because they failed to consider that nation's particularity. They lumped Vietnam into the category of potentially communist states without asking how it stood out within that category. They both ignored what made Vietnam unique and remained oblivious to the mental habits they had adopted when thinking about the problem.

Whether measured in dollars, prestige, influence, or lives, the net effect of this blunder was a stunning, and wholly avoidable, loss of American power and life.

Before the disaster of Vietnam, America confronted even more than the loss of power during the Cuban Missile Crisis. In 1962, the country faced a direct and immediate threat to national security when the Central Intelligence Agency discovered from aerial photography that the Soviets were erecting ballistic missiles in Cuba. The presence of nuclear missiles posed a clear danger because Cuba is merely ninety miles off the Florida coast, and reaction time to an attack would have been negligible. President Kennedy's advisers recognized the danger to American security, but they did not act in reckless haste. They assembled an executive committee to debate the pros and cons of all plausible responses. In the end, rather than launching an all-out air campaign on Cuba to annihilate its offensive capabilities, they chose instead to blockade Cuba and prevent Soviet ships from docking at the island nation. Secretly and simultaneously, President Kennedy authorized a deal with the Soviets. The U.S. would withdraw its aging Jupiter missiles from Turkey, which threatened the Soviets, in exchange for the Soviets withdrawing missiles from Cuba.

Kennedy and his advisers peacefully resolved the Cold War's most precarious conflict by getting beyond a flatview. Earlier scholarship on the crisis described the idea of "groupthink," in which a kind of herd mentality develops within a decision-making body and prevents sober-minded analysis. Groupthink was blamed for the Bay of Pigs fiasco, and the avoidance of groupthink, some believe, is what helped the Kennedy administration to avoid nuclear war over Cuba. That earlier scholarship may be correct, but something more had to be happening for peace to prevail. It was not enough for JFK to avoid being overly influenced by his advisers. The president had to get into the Soviet leaders' minds and acknowledge that not all of them thought alike.

In the tense thirteen days of the Cuban Missile Crisis, one reckless or overly provocative act could have triggered a nuclear war. The air force, led by the aggressive general Curtis LeMay, was itching for a fight. LeMay and his military colleagues wanted to strike at Cuba to eliminate the threat of attack. Some of the military leaders viewed caution as cowardice and patience as weakness. With difficulty Kennedy held them at bay, but their demands for action mounted as each day of the crisis passed.

Kennedy knew that he needed to understand what Soviet premier Nikita Khrushchev was thinking. After all, it was not clear that Khrushchev intended to provoke a war. JFK was able to see that he could not lump all Soviet actions into the category of Soviet aggression. Instead, he looked for nuance within this category, seeking out those elements of their decision-making process that might be more amenable to peace.

One way President Kennedy tried to glean Soviet intentions was by signaling. He in essence communicated with the enemy by probing its responses to various acts. When the first Soviet ships approached the U.S. naval blockade, euphemistically termed a "quarantine," instead of firing on the American vessels, the Soviet ships turned back. When a cabled telegram arrived from the Kremlin, it sounded a conciliatory note. One hour later, a second Kremlin cable arrived stressing a much harder line. It was clear that divisions existed within the Soviet leadership, just as they did on the American side. Kennedy came to believe that Khrushchev did not want to provoke a war over Cuba and that he would be willing to strike a deal. Kennedy, it turned out, was right. The crisis subsided into history as the

nuclear war that wasn't. Averting that war required looking beyond a flatview of Soviet behavior.

Flatviews seem most painful when they cost national power,
prestige, treasure, and above all lives on the massive scale of war.
But flatviews can also cause considerable harm on a much
smaller scale at home. When a flatview affects how we raise
children, it can mar their future. Nations can recover from
blunders they commit, but children can have a harder time as
the victims of an unwitting flatview.

Boys to Men

Mitchell Johnson was thirteen. His friend Andrew Golden was
eleven. On the morning of March 24, 1998, the two boys
headed to their middle school in Jonesboro, Arkansas. Andrew
pulled the fire alarm and ran out to the woods, where Mitchell
was waiting. It was the kind of stunt that kids do sometimes. It
could have been a typical schoolboy prank, but not this time.

As teachers and classmates filed out of the building, Mitchell
and Andrew opened fire. The boys killed four girls and one
teacher while wounding eight others. They tried to escape the
scene but were immediately apprehended by police. The usual
speculation followed. What kind of parents could have allowed
this to happen? Why did the school authorities not recognize
signs of the boys' troubled behavior earlier? Were these just
little monsters? The answers, unfortunately, were frustratingly
thin.

Episodes of school shootings and child killers shock us to the
core, perhaps because we accept that evil acts will be committed
by adults, but eleven years old, we assume, is too young to be so
damaged by circumstances that one could produce so much violence. Many assume that these boys were naturally evil, and

maybe they were. We just don't know for certain. But we do know that although child killers are, thank heaven, extremely rare, too many boys are not dealt with effectively when they are troubled and act out their aggression.

In 1999, two psychologists, Dan Kindlon and Michael Thompson, coauthored a book entitled *Raising Cain*.[13] The authors argue that America, as a society, has so mishandled the emotional lives of boys that it has produced many distant and troubled men. Fathers and mothers, male and female teachers alike, all unconsciously conspire, the authors suggest, to limit the emotional development of boys. As Kindlon and Thompson put it, we want our boys to be "tough" and "strong" based on images of manliness we absorbed from our culture. So when a child is hurting, when he's sad, angry, frustrated, disappointed, or frightened, we don't allow him to learn about what he's feeling. We push him back inside himself with comments like "Just tough it out" or "You need to be strong." The authors contend that we don't teach boys "emotional literacy," the ability to recognize, interpret, and comprehend emotional experiences. As a result, boys not only lack the ability to express their own feelings, they also fail to recognize emotions in others.

Kindlon and Thompson, who have worked for years as school psychologists, describe how teachers and parents reinforce the problems boys have with expressing their emotions. Instead of trying to see each boy as an individual with unique experiences and emotional needs as strong as those of girls, adults tend to react to boys based on archetypal images—the unconscious assumptions about the way all boys are. Although these images limit our understanding of boys, they are widely held by people of intelligence and goodwill.

The archetypes Kindlon and Thompson refer to are just another form of flatview. It is a rigid way of dealing with aggressive boys. People have a prototype of how a boy should be, and they impose it, consciously or not, on the boys in their care. When boys behave violently and act out, we say, "Oh, those boys. That's just how they are." What we should do is ask what is causing this particular boy to act out. Labeling boys as "wild animals" can result in efforts to tame them. Parents and teachers to try to "whip" the wild animals into shape, but the boys' first impulse is not to be controlled, and the situation worsens, if not externally, then internally for the boys. The boys suffer, along with the parents, as well as the people who date and marry them later in life. The authors' underlying point, of course, is that much violence can result from the flatview treatment of children.

Following the Jonesboro massacre, a journalist asked the authors of *Raising Cain* whether the boys who committed the killing were genetically violent or whether the murder had to do with the way the boys were raised. Kindlon and Thompson responded this way:

> We asked her why it is that there is always such an exclusive, determined hunt for a biological culprit. She paused and said, "Well, people are looking for simple answers." But human behavior defies simple explanation, whether we're talking aggression or tenderness. What is clear is that every behavior is influenced by multiple forces, from biology to community. The nature or nurture debate sidesteps the genuine complexity of these issues.

By now, you are probably homing in on the tell-tale signs of cognition traps. From her question, it sounds like this journalist was causefused. She assumed a causal flow from biological imbalance or family dynamic to violent behavior. She assumed a monocausal, reductive explanation. Kindlon and

Thompson deftly sidestepped that cognition trap. At the same time, they saw beyond the flatview of boys. From long years of experience, they recognized that boys have complex emotional lives that are too often crippled by society's rigid categorization of how boys should be. In this case, the result was a killing spree. Most of the time, the damage is hidden far beneath the surface.

Flatviews do damage at the local level, as with the treatment of children, and they hinder prudent policies on the national level, as glaringly occurred in the Cold War. Zoom out now to the global level, and you'll see how flatviews constrict our thinking even about one of the most important issues of our time.

THE FLAT WORLDVIEW

If the Cold War served as a leitmotif in the post–World War II era, today's leitmotif would not be the global war on terror, which affects only a portion of the globe, but globalization, which directly touches the lives of most of the world's inhabitants. Globalization's proponents insist that the process will raise living standards by knitting together the world's economies. When we look at individual well-being around the world, we can find evidence of both rising and falling indicators. Some segments of the Chinese and Indian populations are becoming much wealthier than ever before. At the same time, the number of people living in slums worldwide has skyrocketed. The United Nations estimates that one in six urban inhabitants now resides in a slum: a settlement characterized by the lack of clean drinking water, insecure tenancy, and fragile housing. The UN reports that the number of slum dwellers is increasing by twenty-five million per year. So is globalization succeeding or failing?

The flatview cognition trap locks the globalization debate into a one-dimensional frame. Those who ask only whether globalization is succeeding or not reveal a flat worldview. Some gaze upon all the benefits globalization is bringing to Indian and Chinese software engineers, for example, and conclude that globalization must be a net good for humanity. Others see the growing numbers of slum dwellers as clear evidence that globalization is a net bad. Each side in the debate can find studies supporting its view, but both are caught in a flatview. It is the same kind of flatview that captured Cold War strategic analysts like the Dulles brothers, Robert McNamara, and President Johnson. Those decision makers could not perceive the many dimensions of the foreign leaders they were scrutinizing. Mossadegh was neither all communist, nor all nationalist, nor all authoritarian. He possessed strains of each trait and much more. The same was true of Ho Chi Minh. But the decision makers at the time could see these foreign leaders in only one dimension. When they confronted evidence that contradicted their baseline assumptions about those men, the decision makers subordinated that evidence or dismissed it altogether.

Globalization should be understood as a process operating in many dimensions. It yields benefits for some, misery for others, and can have positive and negative effects on the same people depending on the time period in question. It is creating new middle classes while transforming ancient cultures. It is encouraging innovation in some areas such as computer technology, while stifling creativity in others by homogenizing the products that are produced. It is generating new jobs, enabling some to build fabulous homes while forcing others to live in shantytowns as they flock from villages to cities to compete for the lowest-paid labor available.

It makes more sense to ask whom globalization is good for,

in what ways, and at what time. Globalization is obviously wonderful for the executives of multinational corporations who have seen their salaries, bonuses, and fringe benefits balloon. But it is limiting to these same individuals if they must live within walled, gated, and secured compounds, in cities where they would not be safe to walk freely in the poorer sections. Globalization yields greater varieties of food from which to choose, but simultaneously those foods are diminished in flavor from a global spread of genetically modified crops, or worse, tainted by unsafe production practices in China or other poorly regulated countries. The time horizon matters just as much. The system may be beneficial to some today, but if resentment over globalization's inequities leads to popular mobilization against the rich, they could see their wealth redistributed by peaceful or violent means.

For the poor, globalization is a benefit if it lowers the price of consumer goods, but it's a deficit if those lower prices come at the cost of jobs lost to outsourcing. Viewed in one-dimensional economic terms, the cost savings from cheaper consumer goods might sometimes outweigh the lost wages while workers retrain and search for new employment. But costs in human terms are always multidimensional. When factories close, families can be disrupted if a parent has to travel farther from home to find work. Even if that parent should find a new job at a higher salary than she had before, the costs to the family in time spent away from home could be substantial. Or the time needed to find a new job could be long enough that a marriage breaks under the financial strain. Or others in the community who cannot find new employment might turn to crime, or alcoholism, or domestic violence, all of which have very high costs of their own to the community, but these costs can never be completely measured.

Everyone recognizes that globalization is a complex process, but too many frame the discussion from a flat worldview. If we think about globalization in one-dimensional, flatview terms, we are guaranteed to devise simplistic and ultimately counter-productive policies.

Chapter 4

CURE-ALLISM

Believing That One Size Really Fits All

I N   T H E   L A T E   1960s, Eleanor Rosch, a young Harvard graduate student, set out on a mission to understand how we categorize the world. What she discovered then, and in subsequent
decades of research, was for cognitive scientists a bona fide revolution. Her findings challenged millennia-old beliefs about
how we think, and they corroborated what historians have long
surmised.

To better understand what Rosch discovered, see how
quickly you can respond to the following questions.

A robin is a bird. True or false?

A chicken is a bird. True or false?

An ostrich is a bird. True or false?

Even though all these creatures are birds, Rosch's subjects responded almost immediately to the sentence "A robin is a bird,"
but it took them just slightly longer to answer that a chicken is a
bird. It took them even longer to answer that an ostrich is a bird.

The bird association test might at first glance not seem terribly significant because it is a narrow window into cognition under highly controlled conditions. However, the implications of
this and Rosch's many other similar studies were profound. She
showed that people learn to categorize by best examples. Most
people have in their minds that a robin is more representative of
a bird than an ostrich. In other studies, Rosch found that even

children think this way. They learn good examples of categories earlier than poor ones. Rosch concluded from this and many similar studies that we all tend to think in prototypes, idealized best examples. And it is through prototypes that we form all our categories.

Prototyping, and the cognition traps that result from it, make more sense when we know a bit about how humans categorize information. Our ability to categorize is fundamental. Without it, we could not function. We relate to all objects, events, emotions, and ideas as members of classes. Even our movements are categorized. Categories help us group words, sentences, and even the formation of sounds that allow us to speak. We categorize people, facial expressions, nations, even abstract concepts. Categories are critical in our daily lives, and understanding how we categorize helps us to explain how we reason.

Since the time of Aristotle, the accepted view of categorization assumed that we group things into categories when a group's members share common properties. These categories then form logical sets. In the Greek philosophical worldview, particular experiences that come through the senses were considered unreliable. Because a straight stick looks bent when half is underwater, for example, they believed that we cannot trust our senses to guide our categorization. Instead, only stable, abstract, logical, universal categories could function as objects of knowledge. To fulfill these functions, categories had to be exact, not vague. They had to possess clearly defined boundaries, and their members had to have attributes in common that were the necessary and sufficient conditions for membership in the category. All members of the category had to be equally good with regard to membership; either they had the necessary common features or they didn't. A thing was either inside the category or outside it; there was no in between.

Like many before her, Eleanor Rosch was skeptical about the Greeks' rigid distinctions. Many things do not always fit neatly into clearly defined categories. Rosch was especially interested in colors. Some colors fall between two color categories, like a bluish green. Is one shade of a color a better example of that color than a different shade? Is red hair as good an example of the color red as a fire engine?

When Rosch learned of the Dani, a tribe in the New Guinea Highlands, she realized that they might shed light on her interest in how we conceptualize and categorize the world. The Dani were a Stone Age people whose language possessed only two color terms that corresponded roughly to light and dark. Anthropologists had long debated over whether color categories were arbitrary constructions of culture. Rosch knew that the central members of the basic color categories red, yellow, blue, and green were what are called "unique hue points" in the physiology of color vision. She wondered if these regions might have a special sensory priority. Through her studies of the Highlanders, Rosch established that even though the Dani do not have terms for hues in their language, they were still able to remember central members (the best examples) of standard color categories better than poor examples. She was also able to teach them color names and categories. She found that they could learn names for color categories more easily when the categories were structured around the universal best examples than when the categories were structured unnaturally around peripheral colors. She had the same results when teaching them categories of shapes.

All this led Rosch to suggest a new model for how we create

categories. She asserted that rather than uniformity within categories, where all members are equally good examples of that category, there is actually graded membership in categories, where
some members are better examples than others. She called these
central members of categories prototypes, and her results violated
all the assumptions of the classical view of categorization.

But what about categories that are not just formed from our
perceptions? Is a dentist's chair as good an example of a chair as
a dining room chair? Through much lengthier research, Rosch
established that *all* categories show gradients of membership.

"A German shepherd or a Labrador retriever is a really doggy
dog for people," Rosch told me as we sat in her office at the
base of Berkeley's steep hills. "But a poodle is less prototypi-
cally doggish, and a dachshund is less doggish still. At first, psychologists did not want to accept these findings," she says. "But
eventually the amount of evidence became so overwhelming
that they had to take it seriously—though of course they still
argue and disagree about what the data really mean."

A small, slender woman with graying brown hair and a pen-
sive demeanor, Rosch permits long pauses before she responds
to questions, so that you can almost hear the thoughts churning
in her mind. To me she comes across as a prototypical professor,
though I suspect she'd say that I have a very different best example of a professor in my brain—perhaps an older male with
a tweed jacket, gray beard, and spectacles. When I ask her to tell
me how she came to be a cognitive psychologist, she does not
answer. After a period of silence, she instead tells me a story.

"I'm reluctant to answer that question because I've always
been skeptical about how we construct causal stories in our
lives. I once conducted an informal experiment with our first-
year psychology graduate students. The first-year students have
a seminar where they're supposed to meet the faculty of the

department, and each week a different professor tells them the story of how he or she became a psychologist. It always seemed a little bizarre to me; would one tell the same story to a friend? A potential employer? Your child? A therapist? Yourself? I should confess: I also teach a class in narrative. Anyway, one year when it was my week as speaker, I came in instead with names of all the professions from A to Z, accountant to zookeeper, written on little pieces of paper and had each student pull one out from a hat. I told them that at a signal they were to unfold their paper, assume that they now had the profession or job written on the paper, and then just notice what came to mind. Without exception what happened was that instantly into their mind popped reasons why, of course, they had come to that profession. 'Oh, naturally I'm an architect; I started building little mud castles in the backyard when I was six, and once when a building inspector came around and saw them, he joked about raising our taxes.' 'How could I be anything but a zookeeper? From the time I got Myrtle, my pet turtle, I've always been interested in animals.' 'Being a thief uses all my talents to the maximum the way nothing else could . . .' Each story was hilarious and completely believable both to listeners and teller. I've repeated this demonstration several times, and the only person who ever couldn't do it was one very successful colleague who stated in advance that he could only have become a psychologist. So ask me autobiographical questions at your risk."

Responses such as this revealed a lot about Eleanor Rosch, especially her challenging bent. Her experiment with the students reminds us how, if we are not vigilant, constructed narratives can easily mislead. But it also exposes the foolishness of perceiving someone as an idealized example of her profession.

Prototyping helps to explain why stereotypes are so persistent and why propaganda can be so effective. When we hear the word "bachelor," most of us conjure up an image of a young man living alone, possibly entertaining women in his bachelor pad. The pope is not usually the first image that springs to mind, yet the pope fully fits the formal Aristotelian definition of a bachelor: an unmarried man. Rosch's findings showed that prototypes exist naturally in people's minds, and that they need not be linked to any hard facts. When prototypes have negative social import, we call them stereotypes. Consider the category "welfare mom." An ideal type is immediately created in our heads, even though that image might not at all reflect the most common representative of that category. It shouldn't matter much if birds are represented in our imagination by robins or sparrows, but if our stereotype of a welfare mom is an image of a woman of a particular race and ethnicity and that image arouses a negative emotion in us, then there's reason for concern.

Historians have long recognized the power of prototypes, mainly because the most successful politicians we study are skilled at exploiting them. When Hitler conjured up the image of the Jew, for example, he activated powerful prototypes in the minds of his audience. In fact, when we hear the word "fascist," Hitler is often the first image that comes to mind, even though Mussolini would arguably meet the formal definition of a fascist more accurately, since the doctrine of fascism originated under his rule. The point is that we immediately envision a character like Hitler, not a formal, abstract definition of a fascist. When we hear the word "bird," we don't think, "Hmmm, a beak-nosed, winged creature that lays eggs." Instead, most of us imagine a robin, or another bird like it. Our tendency to think in ideal types is one reason why we are so vulnerable to certain cognition traps. It makes us especially susceptible both to flatview and to cure-allism.

A variant of flatview, cure-allism is a dogmatic belief that a successful theory can be applied indiscriminately. Both cognition traps rely on overly reductive, rigid categorization. But while flatview offers a general perspective on the world, dividing up people, situations, and events into stark, either-or realms, cure-allism is more specific.

Cure-allism is an almost religious belief in a theory's universal applicability. It occurs when we take a theory that has worked well in some cases and we apply it to seemingly similar cases where the theory fails. A new case gets lumped into a category to which it does not belong, and that's when the previously successful theory falls apart. This urge to cram seemingly similar elements into a neatly labeled box might be explained in part by Rosch's research. According to prototype theory, the human mind tends to think in concrete ideal types rather than in rational abstractions. This makes it hard to recognize specificity. We see it happening all around us. Even some of the most gifted minds and top experts in their fields can fall into this trap. And when these converts to cure-allism insist on their theory's universal applicability, the damage can be monumental.

CRAMMING COUNTRIES IN A BOX

Jeffrey Sachs is one of the most noted economists in the world. His academic achievements at Harvard were impressive, even by Harvard standards. It is said that he earned a bachelor's degree, a master's degree, and a Ph.D. before some of his graduate student instructors had completed their own coursework. Sachs's agile mind enabled him to assist Eastern Europe's transition to a market economy following the Soviet Union's demise. But the austere measures (often called "shock therapy") Sachs subsequently prescribed for Russia resulted in an economic fiasco so disruptive that the country is still paying the price to this day.

By the start of the 1990s, Sachs was well placed to tackle one of the most important challenges in his field—guiding the transformation of Eastern European nations from command to free-market economies. Through skillful mastery of a complex situation, Sachs helped the Polish government make that transition with ostensible success, transforming Sachs into an even greater celebrity in his field. With Poland traveling along the right track, it was time to tackle Russia. But just as the country managed to defeat the seemingly unstoppable Napoleon, so too did the harsh Russian climate spoil Sachs's success. This time it was not the cold, but the political, cultural, and historical climate that thwarted Sachs.

Sachs, like many others, had a theory, and it was a good one. He believed that if a communist country privatized state-owned industries, allowing workers to buy shares in these companies, it could move swiftly to a free market. In the Soviet Union, as with communist countries in general, big businesses were owned by the government, not by private individuals like in the United States. Unlike General Motors, America's biggest car manufacturer, which is owned by individuals who hold stock in GM, the Russian car manufacturers were owned by the government. So Sachs and others thought that once the Soviet government and its communist system had collapsed, Russian companies could be sold to private individuals, and their stock shares could be purchased by the workers.

It was a plan that sounded good on paper, but Russia proved corrupt on many levels. Instead of seeing workers gain shares in newly privatized industries, small groups of unscrupulous men managed to buy up the bulk of shares by offering workers a few rubles in exchange for their shares of stock. Why did Russians give away their stocks to greedy oligarchs? Put yourself in their shoes. If you were a Soviet worker and someone offered you a piece of paper representing a share of your formerly state-owned factory, which had always produced lousy products in the past, and someone else offered you real money that you could use immediately to buy food, which would you choose? Not having any experience with stock, but having a lot of experience with endlessly long food lines, you'd probably take the money up front, no matter how little you were being offered. This and many other factors specific to the Russian case made shock therapy "too much shock and too little therapy." The result was what one scholar called the "sale of the century," in which a handful of Russians got magnificently rich and powerful, while millions of previously job-secure workers grew poorer and less secure.

Some of the folks who advocated shock therapy still maintained that it could have succeeded in Russia had it not been for internal corruption and other extenuating circumstances. Of course, it is precisely these extenuating circumstances—the specificity of Russia's case—upon which the theory foundered. One professor of political science at George Washington University called the imposition of shock therapy a "mixture of ignorance and arrogance."[1] Steven Rosefielde, an economics professor at the University of North Carolina, recognized the cognition trap into which the shock therapy advocates had fallen. "There is no scientific theory of how to transform a command economy efficiently into a well-functioning competitive market system . . . The policies they adopted, often called 'shock therapy,' were analogous to removing the control rods from a nuclear reactor, and insisting that the ensuing chain reaction would create a better power system."[2]

Remarkably, some of the best economic thinkers of our age

managed to botch the Russian transition by falling into the cure-allism cognition trap. The economists took a theory that seemed to have succeeded in Poland and other Eastern European countries and assumed it could work in Russia without considering what made the Russian case unique. The shock therapy advocates had latched onto a prototype of postcommunist states and expected Russia to conform to that ideal. In the language of Eleanor Rosch's experiments, Russia was indeed a bird, but more like an ostrich than a robin. The economists forgot that Russians are humans, not numbers in a mathematical equation. They had a distinctive history, culture, and set of experiences that made them unique. The economists squeezed Russia into a box, but the nation refused to fit.

Years later, Sachs reflected on the experience. He insisted that his advice was sound and would have succeeded had it not been for Russia's severe corruption. "Almost nobody in Russia knew anything about democracy or market economy. Unlike Poland, which had national traditions and experience in both, Russia simply lacked the historical knowledge and trained personnel to manage a market economy."[3] Of course, it was exactly this uniqueness that made the cure-all of shock therapy ill-advised. Elsewhere, Sachs acknowledged the blunder, explaining that while Poland enjoyed a robust civil society, fostered by the Catholic Church and the Solidarity movement, Russia possessed a significantly different culture and history, making corruption more disruptive to his theories of economic transformation. "I was overly optimistic about the possibilities of mass privatization," Sachs confessed, "an approach that I now think was flawed, especially when the governments themselves ignored the danger signs of corruption."[4]

While the privatization blunder set back Russia's development, southeast of Russia an entire group of nations was weakened thanks to another economic mishap. Again, cure-allism was partly to blame.

Find and Replace

They called them the Asian "Tigers,"[5] a handful of Asian countries such as South Korea, Singapore, Malaysia, and Thailand who earned the nickname because of their furious growth rates and rising living standards. In the late 1990s the Tigers came under pressure from international institutions to liberalize their financial and capital markets—in other words, to remove their barriers to foreign money. Some countries try to control the amount of money coming into and going out of their nation. They do this because unregulated flows of foreign money can have destabilizing effects on the whole nation. Imagine if you are a Thai entrepreneur and you want to open a large new business. You need to build a factory, hire workers, purchase expensive equipment, and invest a substantial sum up front just to get started. If, instead of going to your local Thai bank for a loan, you raise the money from foreign investors, you will then be dependent on those foreigners to keep their money invested in your company. If they pull out suddenly, your new business will go bust, all those workers will lose their jobs, and everybody suffers. If this happens on a large scale, where many foreign investors suddenly pull out of Thai investments, then the whole country could be affected, causing national unemployment to rise, growth to slow or fall, and poverty to surge. To prevent scenarios like these, countries might restrict or regulate capital flows.

Sometimes, despite the risks, countries decide to relax controls over the flow of foreign money because it can benefit both foreign investors and domestic interest groups. Foreign investors can reap profits from new investment opportunities. Developing countries can profit from new enterprises, which create jobs, raise incomes, and provide revenue from taxation. The people running the International Monetary Fund (IMF)—the international organization that oversees the global financial system—believed that the benefits from liberalized capital markets to both foreign investors and developing countries outweighed the risks, so they pressured some of the Asian Tigers to open up to foreign money.

The IMF had a theory, one that sounded good on paper. If the Tigers could attract more capital from foreign investments, then they could grow even faster than they were already growing. The only problem with this theory was that the East Asian countries didn't need to attract new capital. They already had plenty of money, because their savings rates were remarkably high—in Thailand it was between 30 and 40 percent. The Thais probably would have been better off investing their savings into development projects—upgrading factories, improving education, and building their infrastructure. Instead, by liberalizing their capital markets, they let foreign money flow in, and that money could be withdrawn as swiftly as it appeared.

At the first signs of instability in the Thai economy, international investors wasted no time pulling out. The formerly flourishing Thailand quickly sank into recession. In response, the IMF devised a solution. They had another theory. The IMF looked back to the previous international economic crisis, the Latin American debt crisis of the 1980s, and figured it could apply the same solution to East Asia. It sounded good at first—but there were problems.

Joseph Stiglitz, head of the World Bank at the time of the 1997–98 Asian financial crisis, has been one of the harshest critics of IMF and U.S. Treasury policies. Many of his criticisms are, at their root, commentaries on cognition traps, though not in those words. The problems he describes are examples of cure-allism, with a dash of causefusion thrown into the mix. He points out that the Latin American crisis of the 1980s and the East Asian crisis of the late 1990s had different causes and different contexts. The IMF treated them as if they were the same. Latin America's crisis had been caused primarily by excessively high public deficits and loose monetary policies. "Public deficits" simply means that the governments had spent more than they earned and had to borrow the difference—just like using your credit card to buy something when you don't have enough money in the bank to cover the whole cost. When you try to pay back the credit card debt, the credit card company hits you with interest—a fee they make you pay in exchange for their loaning you the money. Of course, when governments get into debt they can always print more money, but only at the risk of causing inflation. That's an example of loose monetary policy. Monetary policy is one way that a government controls the amount of money in circulation. If it puts too much in circulation, prices rise. Here's why.

Money is just like any other valuable commodity. The scarcer it is, the more it's worth. The more plentiful it is, the less it's worth. If it were raining dollars, for example, dollars would quickly become a nuisance. Everyone would be hiring neighborhood kids to shovel money out of their driveways. If you offered those kids twenty bucks to do the job, they'd laugh you off the block. With dollars just lying around, those kids would immediately raise their fees. You'd either have to pay them more than the amount of dollars in your driveway, or else pay them in some other form. When there's too much money floating around, it loses some of its value. That's why printing too much money (loose monetary policy) doesn't buy happiness, it just brings inflation—a rise in prices to match the plentiful supply of cash.

Now back to Latin America's crisis and how it differed from East Asia's. Expanding the money supply (loose monetary policy) leads to inflation, and in Latin America it led to massive inflation. The IMF's answer then was to impose fiscal austerity: balanced budgets and tighter monetary policies. The Latin American nations were required to pursue these policies if they wanted to receive any further IMF aid. So in 1997, the IMF imposed the same austerity measures on Thailand. There were two principal problems with the IMF's approach. First, the East Asian nations had large budget surpluses, tight monetary policies, and falling inflation—none of Latin America's conditions. The second problem with the IMF's plan was that its austerity program may not even have caused Latin America's recovery, despite what the IMF experts believed.

When the crisis engulfed Indonesia, the IMF fell back on the Mexico analogy, insisting that Mexico had adopted their austerity program of cutting subsidies in the 1980s and came out stronger in the end. This was not only a classic case of cure-allism, it was also a case of causefusion. Mexico's rebound probably occurred not because of austerity measures, but instead because of a surge in oil exports to the United States and the initially positive effects of the NAFTA accord. Indonesia's main trading partner was Japan, which, unlike the U.S., was mired in an economic downturn, unable to buy many Indonesian exports. Despite the uncertainty over the causes of Mexico's recovery, the IMF stuck to its austerity dogma. As conditions worsened for the average Indonesian, the IMF urged a cut in subsidies for basic necessities such as food and fuel, making it extra hard for Indonesians to survive as their real wages were dropping fast. By the summer of 1998 half of all Indonesian firms were either in or near bankruptcy.

Did the IMF economists and those at other international

financial institutions really view all developing countries alike? Stiglitz tells how he heard stories of IMF economists simply copying large portions of their recommendations for one country and pasting them into the report for another. "They might have gotten away with it," he writes, "except the 'search and replace' function on the word processor didn't work properly, leaving the original country's name in a few places."[6]

Not long after, the Asian financial crisis spread to Russia, and the IMF continued applying its theory-bound cure-all. "These economists typically had little knowledge of the history or details of the Russian economy and didn't believe they needed any," Stiglitz charged. "The great strength, and the ultimate weakness, of the economic doctrines upon which they relied is that the doctrines are—or are supposed to be—universal."[7]

Looking back on the crisis ten years later, Stiglitz affirms that capital market liberalization was the wrong prescription. China and India, he points out, are the two main Asian countries that resisted the IMF's plan, and these two nations have enjoyed the most consistent growth rates in the region.[8] The men and women at the IMF and World Bank are smart, good people who have devoted their energies and brainpower to fighting global poverty. Jeffrey Sachs is a good man with the same noble aim. I do not believe that their errors are the result of nefarious plans and selfish ends. Their mistakes stem from their rigid prototypes of market behavior. With those prototypes wedged in place, they unwittingly converted to cure-allism.

PRIVATIZE ME

In the punishing summer heat of 1995, five hundred men in handcuffs traveled by bus from Colorado to a private facility in Texarkana, Texas. As the men filed out, they were met by other men in uniforms. To ensure that the new arrivals would behave, the guards beat them, blasting pepper spray into the eyes of some, prying the lids open to ensure the effects. The guards then crammed twenty-six prisoners into each tiny cell, forcing petty thieves to share space with murderers. Each cell had only one toilet, and the aged plumbing was quickly overwhelmed, causing feces to overflow and prompting a cockroach infestation. The prison itself was nothing more than a converted warehouse. It was not equipped for the brutal East Texas summer heat, which rose above 105 degrees daily. Guards repeatedly beat the inmates, who were not permitted out of their cells for more than one hour per day. Eventually, investigative journalists exposed these conditions and Colorado canceled its contract with the prison. Unfortunately, this case is not a rare exception. It is symptomatic of the abuses occurring within prison corporations.

If any single cure-all has run rampant in America, privatization is it. The privatization form of cure-allism begins in the same way as other forms of the cognition trap. It starts with a theory that works well in many cases, but then it tries to apply that successful theory to areas where it doesn't belong. Governments do tend to be less efficient than private enterprise when it comes to management. As a result, governments have increasingly moved to privatize a wide range of their services. But this theory, as with all forms of cure-allism, becomes a victim of its own success when it morphs into a dogma.

A government's primary responsibility is to its citizens. A corporation's primary responsibility is to its shareholders. Often the interests of shareholders are not compatible with those of the citizens, especially when those shareholders are scattered around the country or the world and the citizens most affected by that corporation's actions are clustered in a small town. The idea of privatizing prisons sounds appealing because it offers state and local governments the possibility of saving money and creating jobs. The flip side is that a private prison has a clear conflict of interest with the larger society. A society should want to see its prison population fall, assuming that criminals are rehabilitated, taught new skills, and assisted with finding jobs once they are released. A private prison, in contrast, has a vested interest in seeing the prison population rise. The more prisoners it can house and the longer it can keep them, the more money it makes, and the greater the returns for its investors. Private prisons have few meaningful incentives to rehabilitate their inmates. On the contrary, they have an incentive to lobby politicians to pass ever tougher laws that will incarcerate ever more people. With those market incentives at work, it is no wonder that corruption has dogged the industry.

In 1994, GEO Group, America's largest private prison corporation, obtained a contract from Coke County, Texas, to open a detention facility for delinquent girls. Construction and operation of correctional facilities is an expensive undertaking requiring capital-intensive investments. In order to get its revenue stream flowing, the company opened the center before it was fully staffed. It had no educational programs, proper medical care, counseling services, or even experienced staff. It was a recipe for disaster. In the lawsuit that followed, plaintiffs charged that girls were "degraded, humiliated, assaulted, harassed, and emotionally abused." Two GEO Group employees later pled guilty to raping some of the girls. On the day that the verdict was reached, one of the victims, a fourteen-year-old girl, committed suicide.

Another GEO Group prison in Austin had its contract canceled after $625,000 in fines were brought against the company for chronic understaffing. The fewer the staff, the lower the operational costs and the greater the profits. Even after the fines were levied, investigators discovered widespread abuses, sexual assaults, drug smuggling, and cover-ups. Twelve employees were indicted on criminal sex charges.[9]

Understaffing as a means of maximizing profits has been a recurrent pattern in private prisons, but understaffing is not the only solution these companies have devised to increase revenues and boost share prices. They have tried eliminating or minimizing services such as medical care, counseling, educational programs, and access to recreation. They have overcrowded their cells, hired inexperienced staff, and cut out rehabilitation. All these cost-cutting measures have most likely been factors in the heightened number of murders, rapes, violence, and poor security in private prisons. Yet many state governments have been eager to privatize their prisons as it lessens a financial burden on the state. One other common cost-saving measure involves sending prisoners across state lines.

On the afternoon of April 27, 2007, several hundred prisoners at a medium-security correctional facility in Newcastle, Indiana, launched a riot. Inmates set fire to mattresses, smashed windows, and injured prison staff and other inmates. Within a few hours, the riot was quelled and security restored. The citizens living nearby the prison, however, had to be concerned. They only learned about the riot once television news crews aired the pictures of a prison courtyard ablaze. Standard procedure in such cases is for the local government to sound alarms and interrupt local broadcasts with the information, allowing neighbors to take precautions in the event of a breakout. But the Newcastle correctional facility is not operated by the government. Instead, it is run by GEO Group, the private corporation that operates the most private prisons across America. Presumably preoccupied with crushing the riot, the company gave the town's residents no warning.

According to GEO Group officials at the prison, newly arrived inmates were upset about the green shirts they were asked to wear. They were also annoyed, company spokesmen said, over the restrictions on tobacco and the smaller portions of food during mealtimes. The prisoners instigating the riot were not from Indiana. They had been transferred there from a facility in Arizona, where prisons are badly overcrowded. The plan was to transfer six hundred of Arizona's inmates to Indiana, which would result in what Indiana's Republican governor, Mitch Daniels, called "pure profit." Indiana would receive additional funds to house these prisoners, and Indianans would be hired to fill the new jobs at the expanded facility. From the governor's viewpoint, it was a win-win situation.

Inmate transfer plans like this one are not uncommon. As overcrowding continues, states with lower prison populations are incentivized to take on inmates from states with an excess. Actually, many states have no other option. Because of mandatory sentencing laws like the Three Strikes legislation, judges are often required to enforce prison sentences regardless of the offender's particular circumstances. As many states' prisons are already overcrowded, the state must either construct new prisons, which voters typically reject on statewide ballot initiatives, or else transfer prisoners across state lines, often to facilities run by private corporations, the two largest being GEO Group and the Corrections Corporation of America.

To minimize the chance of escape, inmates are not informed beforehand that they will be transferred. Instead, they are awakened in the middle of the night, packed onto secure buses, and transported to distant states. These prisoners are not all murderers or rapists. They are also medium- and minimum-security prisoners, guilty of smoking marijuana, petty theft, and other minor crimes. Sometimes violent offenders are placed into lower-security facilities, creating risk to the main prison population, and to local residents in the event of an escape. Beyond these problems, state transfers also remove prisoners from access to their families. Most inmates come from poor and working-class backgrounds. Spouses, partners, and parents are left behind, often to care for children on modest wages. Family visits can be a crucial source of hope for prisoners and their loved ones. But once prisoners are transferred hundreds of miles away, their families cannot afford the cost in transportation and lost wages during the time away from work. Despite GEO Group's assertions, the Arizona inmates in Indiana might have had more cause to riot than just anger over their green shirts.

It's easy to assume that greed is a major factor fueling the expansion of private prisons. The potential profits for shareholders are large, and many other industries benefit as well. Companies can lock up extremely lucrative contracts to supply private prisons with soap, cleaning supplies, uniforms, food, and similar goods. But greed is only one factor. There is a plausible case to be made for private prisons. One advantage is that they are newer and can sometimes be cleaner than the many aging government-run detention centers. Some prisoners in some studies have said that they prefer being housed in these newer private prisons. But despite their modern facades, private prisons exist on inherent conflicts of interest. They demand some kind of philosophical justification or the public could never accept them. That rationalization comes from our belief in cure-allism.

Again, privatization is often the best way of making inefficient government-run industries more effective, but it is not always the right course. In Russia, unregulated privatization of firms dramatically skewed the distribution of wealth. In America, privatizing prisons has encouraged prison populations to rise, allowed abuses to occur from inadequate regulation, and sapped the justice system's already flaccid efforts at rehabilitation.

Markets are believed to be immensely powerful, and they are. Market forces are strong, but they are powerful in both directions. They can be harnessed for good or ill. Victims of cure-allism convince themselves that privatization is always positive, no matter where the theory is applied. They think it has the power to solve all our social ills. It is exactly that indiscriminate use of the theory that can make our problems worse. When privatization is implemented prudently, it can benefit corporations and their clients alike. Two cases of privatizing water in Bolivia demonstrate how businesses can either rob themselves of profits when they convert to cure-allism or maximize their profits by resisting the cure-all dogma.

For the South American nation of Bolivia the new millennium began in protest and fear. The unrest began in Cochabamba and quickly spread to cities around the country. Protesters blocked highways and manned barricades, throwing rocks and Molotov cocktails at government security forces. Police responded with tear gas and rubber bullets. On April 8, police fired into a crowd, striking seventeen-year old Víctor Hugo Daza in the face and killing him. Daza's death did not cow the protesters; it only inflamed them further. The target of their anger was not just the government, but the corporate executives of the San Francisco–based Bechtel corporation.

The previous year the World Bank had refused to issue loans to Bolivia unless that nation privatized its water system. Bolivia's water service was inefficient and riddled with corruption. World Bank theory insisted that privatization would cure the problem. When the water system was auctioned off, Bechtel was the only bidder. Though it was valued at millions, Bechtel purchased the rights to operate Cochabamba's system for just $20,000. The concession guaranteed Bechtel a 15 percent annual return on its investment, adjusted each year to correspond to the United States' consumer price index (the index that measures inflation). Revamping Cochabamba's water system would be costly and capital-intensive. The first thing the corporation did in January 2000 was raise rates across the board by an average of 35 percent. Most Cochabambans earned approximately $70 a month. With the Bechtel rate hike, many now had to pay $20 a month for running water. It was a burden that the poor could not, and would not, bear.

Led by the fiery Oscar Olivera, the protesters demanded that the Bechtel contract be revoked. Cochabambans, they insisted, had never been asked whether they wanted their water privatized. They viewed affordable access to this natural resource as a right and the people's control over it as integral to a democracy. The government responded with a heavy fist. It jailed many of the protest leaders, sending them to remote jungle prisons. None of the harsh tactics succeeded in quelling the growing unrest. When police told Bechtel executives that they could no longer ensure their safety, the executives fled, and Bolivia's president, Hugo Bánzer Suárez, was forced to back down. Banzer canceled the contract and returned control of Cochabamba's water to the local government. In 2006, Cochabamba's water service was still inefficient, still corrupt, and still failed to service many of the residents. The rates, however, had fallen back to their pre-2000 levels.

Around the same time that Cochabamba privatized its water system, Bolivia's capital, La Paz, did the same, but with a very different result. La Paz contracted with the French Suez Corporation, which adopted a significantly different approach to the problem of cost. The Suez subsidiary decided to hold rates constant for the first five years of its operations. Residents would not have to pay any more for their water during those five years than they had before privatization. After this initial period ended, the company introduced a fee structure based on consumption. They eliminated the flat fees that had previously existed and instituted a system where the more water people used, the more they paid. The company profited because the average price of water actually rose by 38 percent, but it fell for the poorest one third of customers. The poorest citizens of La Paz, it turned out, were also the most frugal. They did not need to use as much water as wealthier citizens, who owned washing machines and dishwashers and took long showers. In effect, the wealthier residents were subsidizing the poorer ones, and in this way nearly everyone who wanted water could get it. Suez was able in a relatively short time to recoup its investment, increase service to 90 percent of the city's residents (exceeding the 77 percent target), and enable water rates for the poorest residents to fall. Unlike in Cochabamba, where residents were paying $20 a month for water, La Paz's residents paid an average of just $1.90 per month.

These two cities' stories of water privatization tell us something about how cure-allism can be overcome. Privatization goes wrong when it is implemented indiscriminately. Some services, like prisons, should never be privatized because the conflict of interest is too great. Water systems may not always be like that. They might be privatized effectively as long as there is regulation, oversight, and, most important, a distinction made among consumers. Bechtel saw all Cochabambans as the same, with the same ability to pay its increased fees. The result was that the poor, who were hit hardest, revolted. They compelled the president to nullify Bechtel's contract and forced its executives to flee the country. It was a classic blunder: Bechtel's solution to the problem of capital outlays—raising fees across the board—completely backfired, ultimately undermining the company's hopes of netting big profits. Suez, on the other hand, recognized that its consumers were in differing economic circumstances. By eliminating the flat fee and instead charging for consumption, the company surpassed the city's objective of extending access to clean water and at the same time turned a profit. Unfortunately, the company later became dissatisfied with the returns on its investment and began to alter its fee structure. Protests followed. Water privatization remains an ongoing issue, but one element that can help smooth the process is for companies to discern nuance within the category of "consumer."

Historians or social anthropologists might have been able to tell Bechtel that their fee structure was unwise. One of the most problematic features of colonialism involved the flat-fee taxation system that the Europeans imposed on their colonies. Before colonization many societies used a kind of progressive tax system. Local village headmen decided how much to charge each household based on its individual circumstances. If one family had lost a son or suffered some hardship that reduced their income that year, a fair-minded headman might charge that family less. A household that enjoyed a bumper crop might be charged more. When the Europeans came, they tended to charge a flat per-head tax, where every villager was forced to pay the same amount regardless of his circumstances. This system created vastly more destitute people than had existed before. Bechtel's flat-fee rate hikes threatened to have a similar effect, whereas Suez's more flexible pricing scheme enabled the wealthier to subsidize the minimal water usage of the poor. The plan was not just empathetic, it was in Suez's long-term interest.[10]

International development programs have been criticized from just about every angle. Donors complain that the money is often wasted. Recipients object to having their autonomy infringed by all the strings attached to World Bank and IMF loans. And antidevelopment protesters charge that the aid is just a modern form of economic imperialism intended to underdevelop the poor and enrich the elite. Greed, corruption, and politics are never far from the scene when massive amounts of money are involved. But there has to be more to the story than that. In a thoughtful study of large-scale state-sponsored development projects, the anthropologist James Scott put his finger on a common flaw in most aid efforts. He found that experts regularly ignore their subjects. "What is striking, of course," Scott writes, "is that such subjects . . . have, for the purposes of the planning exercise, no gender, no tastes, no history, no values, no opinions or original ideas, no traditions, and no distinctive personalities to contribute to the enterprise."[11] While theories are a necessary aspect of planning, their true danger comes when we forget how often individuals, businesses, and nations defy the prototypes we assign them.

Theories, just like categories, are essential in our daily lives. It would be impossible to function without them. Theories are not harmful in themselves. It is only the mindless adherence to any given theory of human nature that is unwise and that can lead to great misfortune. Cognition traps like cure-allism prevent us from seeing specificity—individual, cultural, or historical. They make us forget that human beings are complex and that no single theory of their behavior will always hold true. They keep us from discerning relevant distinctions within categories. In short, they make us think in prototypes, idealized best examples that seldom appear in real life. Cure-allism is so seductive because it usually begins with theories that work, and work well, on certain problems. Applying those theories where they don't belong is what can impoverish whole nations and ruin lives.

Chapter 5

INFOMANIA

The Obsessive Relationship to Information

MATHILDE LOISEL WAS born beautiful but middle class. She longed for a life of leisure in Parisian high society, but her prospects were few. She married a clerk in the Ministry of Public Instruction. Then one night her husband surprised her with an invitation to an elite affair. Mathilde burst into tears. She knew she owned nothing fine enough to suit the occasion. Her husband suggested her theater gown, which only made Mathilde cry even harder. To her delight, her husband offered to spend the few hundred francs he had saved on a new gown. A few days later Mathilde realized that she had no jewelry for the event, and so she asked a wealthy friend if she could borrow her dazzling diamond necklace.

Mathilde outshone every other woman that evening. Every man asked her to dance; everyone wanted to know her name. It was the night she had dreamed of. But when they returned to their modest apartment, Mathilde discovered that the necklace was gone. Somehow she had lost it on the way home. Frantically her husband retraced their steps and found nothing. Resigned to what they had to do, the couple found an identical necklace, which they purchased for thirty-six thousand francs. For the next ten years Mathilde and her husband worked every menial job they could get to pay off their exorbitant debt. Mathilde washed soiled linens, cleaned clothes, and made herself a servant in wealthier homes. The hard labor aged them both, but after ten years the debts at last were paid. Then one day in the Champs-Élysées, Mathilde saw her old friend who had loaned her the necklace. The friend could no longer recognize her. Mathilde explained how she had worked for a decade to pay back the cost of the jewelry. Her friend was shocked. If she had only known what Mathilde intended, she could have told her then what she told her now. It was barely worth five hundred francs. The necklace was a fake.

By now you've read enough of this book to know that this fictional tale embodies another cognition trap. Guy de Maupassant's short story shows how even friends can suffer from infomania. Infomania is the information-based cognition trap, a condition marked by an obsessive relationship to information. Infomaniacs believe that if they can control the knowledge around them, they will profit. But more often the opposite occurs, and infomaniacs unwittingly defeat themselves. There are two types of infomaniacs. The first are the infomisers, those who hoard information, believing that sharing their data will undermine their position. They hog information to themselves or their closest coterie, controlling it so tightly that they never share it with others who might help them avoid potential blunders. The other type of infomaniacs, the infovoiders, believe that sealing themselves off from information to keep themselves in an information void will somehow be to their benefit. I'll say more about the infovoiders a bit later. For now, let's focus on the infomisers.

In "The Necklace," both friends withheld vital information from each other. The wealthier woman should have told Mathilde that her necklace was only costume jewelry. Mathilde should have told her friend that she had lost the necklace and intended to replace it. But of course if they had done this it wouldn't make nearly as good a story. Infomisering makes for terrific fiction, but it's much easier to read about its effects than to have to live with them.

At its core, infomisering occurs when people convince themselves that their positions are threatened if knowledge is spread. In Mathilde's case, she feared what her friend would think if she knew the truth about her carelessness with the necklace. Attempting to safeguard her perceived position as a reliable woman, Mathilde destroyed her position through needless sacrifice. Of course, infomisering is not merely a feature of intimate relationships. It is especially prevalent in complex organizations like governmental bureaucracies and large corporations. Sometimes infomisers think that their agendas, or even their very jobs, could be at stake if colleagues get hold of important data and use it to undermine them. At other times infomisering stems from hubris, an arrogant assumption that the infomiser knows best. He believes that his plans are so superior to anyone else's that sharing information with others could only waste time or bring trouble. Even in intimate relationships, infomisers withhold vital secrets from partners or friends, fearing that their relationship might be jeopardized if others knew the full story. Obviously, some secrets should always be kept, and some information is imprudent to share. What distinguishes an infomiser is his failure to recognize those times when sharing information could help avert disaster. He overestimates the benefits from infomisering and discounts the value of his friends' or colleagues' potential wisdom.

THE COMMANDER WHO LOST HIS TROOPS

Imagine for a moment that you are in command of an army corps. Your orders are to defend the homeland at all cost. If you fail, you will most likely be killed either by invading forces or by your own authoritarian regime. Now imagine that your every command decision, your every order, is scrutinized by an intricate web of spies, all working for your own government and assigned to spy on you. Some of these spies are there simply to spy on the other spies around them. Not only are all your communications monitored, but you are forbidden to maintain any friendships with fellow commanders because your nation's leadership fears this sort of familiarity could facilitate a coup. And to make your job just a bit more challenging, you are forbidden even to communicate with other units, upon whom you depend for coordinating your movements. When the invasion comes, how do you think you might function?

Saddam Hussein's military operated under precisely these impossible constraints because Saddam was an infomaniac. Thanks to the work of the U.S. Joint Forces Command Operational Analysis team, military historians have conducted interviews with some two hundred Iraqi officers and reviewed several thousand pages of captured documents. What these sources reveal is a degree of infomisering worthy of a Guinness record. One Republican Guard commander of I Corps explained to American officials, "I was completely uninformed about other unit plans around me. I had the Al Nida and the Baghdad divisions but officially I could not ask them about any of their missions and plans that were sent to them directly from Republican Guard headquarters in Baghdad."[1] The I Corps commander revealed the true absurdity of Saddam's obsessive need to control the information flow. The commander admitted that because he was not permitted to communicate with sister units, he often had to run reconnaissance over his own battlefield just to discover where the other Iraqi units were located.

Another military officer, the commander of II Corps, explained that in order to establish some semblance of coordination with others, he held meetings inside the walled garden of a private home where he believed the security services could not eavesdrop on him. Since every directive had to come ultimately from, or be in line with, the wishes of Saddam or his son Qusay, a commander who deviated from those instructions risked more than his career.

Infomisers exist in every organization and every government. Part of their motivation for hoarding data stems from a gnawing paranoia that if others possess information, they will use it against them. Intensive infomisering is a hallmark of dictatorships, and it is usually to the infomiser's detriment. If, for example, Saddam had permitted a freer flow of information, his troops would undoubtedly have performed more successfully. But the fear of being overthrown is not the only motivation for infomisers. Sometimes infomisers act out of ambition, fearing that if information is shared, then others might advance their careers at the infomiser's expense. And sometimes they hoard information in the hope of keeping their colleagues ignorant and unable to undermine their policy objectives. Yet whether it occurs in governments, businesses, or personal relationships, too much infomisering tends to backfire. And when the stakes are sufficiently high, it can spell the difference between war and peace.

The Minister of Manipulation

In the spring of 1893, a ship docked in Portland, Oregon, and off-loaded an unlikely cargo. On board stood a thirteen-year-old boy, a subject of the distant empire of Japan. He had been at sea for weeks, without parent or guardian. As passengers disembarked, embraced their loved ones, and gradually passed from view, the boy continued to wait. He was expecting to be met by a relative who had agreed to care for him, but that relative never appeared. It was an inauspicious welcome to a new world. Yet the young boy would find his way, gaining an education, a law degree with top honors, and a putatively keen knowledge of America. Despite that knowledge, it was Yosuke Matsuoka who, as Japan's foreign minister, would guide his nation into the Axis alliance and propel his country toward war. Along the way, he would develop into a skilled infomiser, believing that information control would advance both his career and his policies.

Once forced open to trade by U.S. commodore Matthew Perry in 1853, Japan set about industrializing in Western fashion. It not only adopted Western technology and the weapons of modern war, it also adopted the accoutrements of democracy: limited parliamentary government, partial enfranchisement, and a constitution. Unfortunately for Japan, it chose a Prussian model for its constitution. Though there are numerous reasons why Japan's experiment with democracy failed, the country followed a course vaguely similar to that of Germany in the 1930s. In both nations, militarism rose, parliamentarianism broke down, and dictatorship ensued. Yet it was never inevitable that Germany and Japan, oceans apart and with few links to bind them, should have come to unite in the original Axis of Evil. That union occurred in good part because of one man's assiduous efforts.

Steering his country into the arms of Nazi Germany was not a simple task. To pull off what he believed would be a diplomatic coup, Matsuoka had to overcome stiff resistance within his government. Throughout the 1930s, before his elevation to foreign minister, Matsuoka traveled widely across Japan, holding public lectures on his views for the nation's future foreign and domestic policies. He advocated the dissolution of political parties and stressed the need for close cooperation between Japan, Germany, and Italy.[2] It was during this time that he served as president of the South Manchuria Railway Company, a keystone in Japan's expansion onto the mainland. Revealing his pomposity and flare for the grandiose, Matsuoka authored a book about the railway, stating in its preface:

> In my little book I have done my best to present clearly and honestly the remarkable change that has come over the face of Manchuria during the single generation that has elapsed since Japan set her first courageous foot there, and the South Manchuria Railway was founded. Until that moment, which is likely to prove one of the most significant moments in modern history, Manchuria had lain for countless centuries a bare, undeveloped, and sparsely populated land.[3]

Matsuoka called Japan's role in Manchuria "a subject that is of supreme importance to all the world."[4]

Although Japanese foreign policy in the 1930s and throughout the war was decidedly expansionist, it did not go unchastened. When in 1938–39 the Japanese Kwantung Army attempted to expand its dominion beyond its puppet state of Manchuria, which the Japanese had renamed Manchukuo, Japanese forces suffered a stunning defeat at the hands of Soviet troops. General Georgy Zhukov's victory was so decisive that it earned him the title "Hero of the Soviet Union." In the wake of that defeat, Japanese leaders soberly chose to expand elsewhere. An alliance with Nazi Germany offered a tempting prize. Japan could piggyback on German conquests by gobbling up the Far Eastern colonies of Germany's defeated European foes. But this policy risked potentially greater losses by instigating a conflict with the United States. Despite the risks, Matsuoka spearheaded a campaign to ally with Hitler's regime.

Upon his appointment as foreign minister in 1940, Matsuoka set his plans in motion for reaching accord with the Third Reich. The Axis alliance represented part of his broader conception of Japan's role in a new world order and of Germany's ascension. At the Japanese cabinet liaison conference on September 16, 1940, when the pact with Germany was discussed, Matsuoka and General Hideki Tojo had to gain cabinet support for the Axis alliance. Since all cabinet members understood that an Axis alliance would make Japan an enemy of America, both men needed to heighten their colleagues' anti-American sentiments. Tojo, who was at the time war minister, contended that American economic support of China's Chiang Kai-shek regime had prevented Japan from completing its conquest of China.[5] This was a clever ploy, for Tojo and Matsuoka recognized that victory over China was a primary concern. Every Japanese cabinet since 1937 had made it a top priority, but none had managed to subdue Chinese resistance. Tojo and Matsuoka exploited Japanese frustration over the China quagmire by using America as the scapegoat for Japan's failure.

Blaming the United States was one among many subtle acts of infomisering. Matsuoka was well aware that American aid to China made little impact. Only two weeks prior to the September 16 conference, Matsuoka noted in a diplomatic cable that the Chinese had requested a loan of $25 million from the United States, but received only a meager $3 million.[6] Though he knew how little funding the Chinese resistance received from the U.S., Matsuoka manipulated his colleagues by withholding this information and attempting to create the opposite impression, that American intervention was pivotal in keeping

the Chinese resistance alive. It was one of many acts of infomisering intended to facilitate the alliance with Hitler's Third
Reich. Matsuoka believed he could control the information
flow enough to manipulate people and events. But he forgot
the human factor. Most people resent acts of information control, and they will often retaliate in kind. This is precisely what
occurred when his colleagues at last turned the tables on him.
But by then the damage to Japanese-American relations had
been done.

By late June 1941, American secretary of state Cordell Hull's
line had begun to harden. In consecutive proposals on June 21
and 22, Hull outlined American desires to see Japan end its war
in China and divorce itself from the Axis. At this late date, however, Hull's demands seemed implausible to the Japanese. After
four years of military commitment in China, no Japanese cabinet could withdraw and expect to remain in power. Withdrawal
from the Axis was equally unlikely from Japan's standpoint. The
Axis alliance offered the hope of Japan's "New Order" in East
Asia, of which Matsuoka and Tojo had been principal architects. Germany's defeat of Holland and France left those countries' colonial possessions defenseless. Without the German
alliance, these men feared that the southward expansion and ex-
tension of Japanese hegemony in East Asia would be jeopardized. Surprisingly, despite Hull's demands, only Matsuoka
called for an end to Japanese-American talks.

At a cabinet conference on July 2, 1941, Matsuoka insisted
that the Hull proposals could not be accepted and pushed for an
end to negotiations. But his cabinet colleagues were not as certain. That same evening, Prime Minister Fumimaro Konoye
held a secret meeting with the army, navy, and home ministers
to discuss Matsuoka's aggressive posture toward America. None
of the participants wished to provoke the United States. The

subsequent debate on July 12 revealed that Matsuoka stood alone in his zeal to abandon peace. Army Chief of Staff Sugiyama declared that although he agreed with Matsuoka's opinion of the Hull proposals, "we among the military believe it is appropriate on this occasion to leave room for negotiation."[7] Home Minister Kiichiro Hiranuma urged that the talks be continued. Hiranuma reasoned that "it would seem that we must avoid a break with the United States from the standpoint of the Empire's survival."[8]

Under pressure from his colleagues, Matsuoka agreed to reject Hull's demands, but to simultaneously send a Japanese counterproposal, so as not to give Hull the impression of Japanese intransigence. The military leaders were not yet ready to burn their bridges with America. They still did not realize that Matsuoka suffered from infomania. Matsuoka assured his fellow ministers, "Japanese-American accord has been my cherished wish ever since I was young. I think there is no hope, but let us try until the very end."[9] His words would soon ring hollow.

Matsuoka now engaged in one final and ultimately deadly act of infomisering. Flouting his government's instructions, he wired only the rejection to Hull without also sending the counterproposal. He was playing a game of brinkmanship, expecting that by selectively hoarding information, he could manipulate events as he hoped. But infomisering breeds retaliation. One of Matsuoka's subordinates, Hidenari Terasaki, chief of the Japanese Foreign Ministry's American bureau, detected Matsuoka's covert maneuver. Sensing the critical implications of these communications, Terasaki acted on his own authority and wired the counterproposal to Washington. But meanwhile, Matsuoka secretly informed the Germans of Japan's reply to Hull.[10] With these actions Matsuoka vastly overstepped the limits of his authority.

Matsuoka simply had to go. But rather than dismissing him, Konoye resigned his entire cabinet and reassembled it two days later with exactly the same personnel, save for Matsuoka. Since Matsuoka had been the most public advocate for the Axis, Konoye and the other ministers hoped that by removing him, Japan could demonstrate its desire to continue negotiations with the United States. All the while, preparations for Pearl Harbor would move forward, just in case. But Washington could not discern Konoye's opaque intentions. The damage Matsuoka had done to what was already a tenuous relationship proved irreparable.

American ambassador to Japan Joseph Grew had long believed that Matsuoka was intent on peace with the U.S., against the wishes of the Japanese military. Upon more sober reflection in the wake of deteriorated Japanese-American relations, and just nineteen days before Pearl Harbor, Grew at last revised his opinion of Matsuoka's machinations. In his diary, Grew wrote:

> Have often thought about my letter to Prince Konoye in reply to his letter informing me of the fall of his cabinet, and my allusion to the distinguished service he rendered his country. Some people might quibble at that statement, on the ground that he led his country into all sorts of difficulties, including the Axis alliance. I grant all that, but I put it down more to the nefarious influence of Matsuoka than to Konoye himself, who had his own military people and extremists to deal with.[11]

Had Matsuoka allowed the free flow of information, had he recognized that infomisers breed deception, distrust, and subversion, Japan's fate in World War II might have been different. Matsuoka alone cannot be blamed for Pearl Harbor, but his infomisering substantially contributed to the destruction of Japanese-American relations. Once diplomacy with the U.S. was no longer an option, Japan's fateful decision for Pearl Harbor progressed unchecked. Japanese-American relations recovered only after a brutal and bloody war, the dropping of two atomic bombs, American occupation of the home islands, and a fundamental reshaping of Japanese society.

KILLER COGNITION

There is a type of fear that is so intense that it paralyzes. Like in a dream, you want to scream, but no sound will come. You want to run but cannot move. It must have been the damp, swamplike ground that muffled his approach. Slowly, deliberately, a large, thickset man in boots and a windbreaker moved toward them. Cecelia spotted him first. Then Bryan saw he was carrying a gun and a length of rope. As he neared, Bryan recognized one other disturbing feature. The man's head was completely covered in a black hood with slits for the eyes and mouth. The effect was of a medieval executioner. The man explained, calmly, softly, that he would have to tie them up. At gunpoint, they complied. And then the man raised a large knife above Bryan's body and thrust it repeatedly into his back. Next he turned on Cecelia, stabbing her in the breasts, stomach, and groin. Slowly, he walked away.

Amazingly, the two were not dead. Though the ropes were slippery with their blood, Bryan managed to untie Cecelia's binding with his teeth, and she then untied him. Bryan crawled to a road, was spotted by passersby, and both were rushed to the emergency room. Cecelia died a few days later. Bryan survived, but he could not identify the attacker. Though they never saw his face, the killer left ample clues to his code name. Zodiac had struck again.

Zodiac's case remains one of the great unsolved episodes in American crime history. His ten-month killing spree in the late 1960s terrified the Bay Area and may even have continued through the mid-1970s, though later killings could not be definitively confirmed as his crimes. Aside from being a grisly tale of sadism, violence, and terror, the Zodiac nightmare also provides a chilling example of the dangers of infomisering. Multiple law enforcement agencies frequently failed to share critical information with each other—information that might have led to the killer's capture. Sometimes this infomisering was inadvertent, and sometimes it was actively pursued as a matter of policy. One sign of the killer's intelligence is that he often committed his crimes in areas where agencies had overlapping jurisdictions, correctly perceiving that territorial disputes and police infomisering would buy him more time to kill.

Infomisering is more than just a tactic used to advance one's career. It is also a way of approaching problems. Infomisers think that they alone are best equipped to run the show. Allowing others into the information loop, they believe, would only muddy the waters and make it harder to accomplish their goals. Obviously, compartmentalizing information is sometimes essential. Protecting national security or individual privacy often requires keeping information secret except from a necessary few. The foolishness of infomisers is that they fail to recognize when a problem can be solved faster or smarter, or possibly even prevented when relevant others are involved. We may still not yet be certain whether the 2007 killing spree at Virginia Tech, the most deadly school shooting in American history, could have been averted if information about the troubled young student had been shared with school officials. Societies must always weigh the costs of stigmatizing the mentally ill against protecting the community from possible harm. However, the Virginia Tech Review Panel established by Governor Timothy Kaine found that key university health officials were not informed about the killer's serious and long-standing psychological condition.

On a national scale, the most notable case of infomisering involves the failure of FBI and CIA officials to share with each other critical data about the 9/11 hijackers. President Bush created the Directorate of National Intelligence in order to end institutionalized infomisering. Whether this new and cumbersome bureaucratic structure can successfully combat infomisering will depend in part on DNI staff's ability to avoid infomisering among themselves. And it will also depend on all U.S. intelligence agencies resisting the other major form of infomania—infovoiding: the active shunning of unwanted information.

THE INFOVOIDERS

Bishop Diego de Landa was a man with a mission. His job was to bring religion to the conquered, but his methods were less than charitable. Following the Spanish conquest of Yucatán in the mid-1500s, de Landa set out into the flat, dry lands of Mexico to convert the Mayan natives to Christianity. Like most of the European explorers and missionaries, he viewed Mayan religious practices as pagan. In order to turn them away from their savage ways, de Landa used a process called hoisting. After a victim's hands were bound, his body was suspended from a tree. Stone weights were tied to his ankles, and the victim was whipped on the back. After this, the interrogation began. De Landa's own records reveal that both the Spanish soldiers and the missionaries adopted the Council of Cleon, exerting excessive force against their subjects when it was not necessary. But Diego de Landa also suffered from a form of infomania called infovoiding.

Infovoiding is another type of infomania. Unlike the infomisers, who hoard information for themselves, infovoiders do exactly the opposite. Caught in this mind-set, infovoiders believe that obsessively avoiding information can actually help them achieve their goals. Rather than confronting vital information about their situation, infovoiders instead shun the very data that could keep them safe from blunders. In the process, they not only sabotage their missions, they often undermine the goals of their colleagues, organization, or country.

Although the Spanish invaders did not view it this way at the time, anthropologists today believe that the Mayan culture contained one of the most advanced civilizations in the New World. On the one hand, they practiced human sacrifices and brutal killings—things we would by our contemporary standards consider primitive acts. On the other, they organized their society in complex ways. Mayan cities were extremely well ordered. City centers were marked by temples, which were surrounded by the homes of priests and chiefs, in turn surrounded by homes of the wealthier inhabitants, and finally commoners living on the towns' borders. City grounds were well kept and tree lined. Among the many indications of a complex society, one of the most striking was the Mayan texts.

While traveling in the city of Mani, de Landa discovered something completely unexpected. The sixteenth-century Mayans had developed an intricate written language. Carefully constructed scrolls recorded details of their science and religion. These books contained a series of symbols that not only provided invaluable information on their religious rituals and accumulated knowledge; they also provided a Rosetta stone for decoding the Mayan tongue. As a body of knowledge, these books held keys to deciphering a vast and fascinating civilization. They were an astonishing find.

On July 12, 1562, de Landa ordered that all Mayan written records be burned. Five thousand idols and at least twenty-seven books of Mayan hieroglyphs were immolated. The auto-da-fé, a Spanish ritual of burning heathen artifacts (and sometimes the nonbelievers themselves), irrevocably removed the best hope of accessing Mayan culture. Once burned, this font of knowledge was lost forever. It was an excruciating act of infovoiding.

To de Landa, of course, the Mayan texts were a trove, but not a treasure. In his account of the book burning, de Landa wrote: "Thus they venerated each *katun* [an idol] for twenty years, and during ten years they governed themselves by their superstitions and deceits, all of which were so many and such as to hold in error these simple people, that one would have to marvel over it who did not know the things of Nature and experience the devil possesses in dealing with them." His entire reference to the book-burning episode is condensed into these few sentences: "These people also used certain characters or letters, with which they wrote in their books about the antiquities and their sciences; with these, and with figures, and certain signs in the figures, they understood their matters, made them known, and taught them. We found a great number of books in these letters, and since they contained nothing but superstitions and falsehoods of the devil we burned them all, which they took most grievously, and which gave them great pain."[12]

Shortly after the auto-da-fé, Bishop Toral, de Landa's superior, arrived in Yucatán. Recognizing that de Landa had gone too far, he released the Mayan prisoners and ordered de Landa back to Spain to stand trial for his actions. Assessed by a jury of his peers, de Landa was acquitted of all crimes, but his mission to Mexico was at an end.

The bishop believed that he was doing God's work by annihilating pagan texts, but he was actually sabotaging his own mission. Infovoiding placed de Landa and his cadre in a partial information vacuum about the people he was meant to be converting. If de Landa had translated the scrolls, studied them, and learned how the Mayans thought about their gods, he could have been more successful at converting them. Armed with rich information about their religion, culture, and science, de Landa might have devised powerfully effective strategies to win souls for Christ. Instead, he shunned this information and weakened his position. At the same time, he made conversions more difficult for the missionaries who would replace him.

CLOSED PORTS, CLOSED MINDS

"The English are cunning and deceitful," the new emperor declared. "They are not of our race, and so their minds are completely different from ours. They should not be allowed to reside here."[13]

When a British emissary pressed the newly unified Vietnamese state for permission to establish a factory at Da Nang, Emperor Gia Long flatly refused. He not only rejected foreign requests for an audience, he even spelled out his rationale: "When the former kings governed the state, they did not let the civilized mingle with the barbarians." Gia Long's rigidity was not absolute, for he did integrate a handful of European military advisers into his court. The true surge in xenophobia came with his successors. Their policy of infovoiding magnified their country's troubles, fostering their subjugation and instability over the course of the next two centuries.[14]

At the close of a protracted civil war that pitted several powerful families against each other, the Nguyen (pronounced "nwin") clan emerged victorious at the start of the nineteenth century and established their rule over a united Vietnam. Gia Long, the first Nguyen emperor, took his name from the old forms of two major cities, one in the north, the other in the south—Saigon and Hanoi. It was a symbolic gesture of national unity. But forging internal cohesion was not Gia Long's only challenge. The European colonizers were eager to make inroads into Vietnam, not only through trade, but through religious conversions as well, a process that Nguyen rulers viewed as subversion. In confronting the European danger, Nguyen emperors were hamstrung in part by infovoiding.

From an outsider's perspective, it can seem hard to understand why people sometimes choose to avoid information that could improve their decisions. In Bishop de Landa's case, he had a conviction that his own religious beliefs were inherently superior to those of the Mayans. The Mayans, he reasoned, had nothing to offer him. In the Nguyen case, their infovoiding similarly stemmed partly from a sense of superiority, one enhanced by a historical and cultural tradition. The Nguyen had adopted the Chinese civil administration model. Because Nguyen rulers patterned their governmental practices along Chinese lines, they embodied the Confucian outlook, which viewed the emperor as a son of heaven. This meant that the emperor was considered, and he considered himself, as superior to all others in judgment. He assumed that by virtue of his position, he naturally attracted the respect of foreigners. With the exception of China, all other countries were ranked according to a strict hierarchy, all of them, of course, ranking below Vietnam. Foreign ambassadors and envoys were therefore expected to behave like vassals and to accord the emperor the deference his vaunted stature demanded. The powerful Europeans, however, were less inclined toward this view.

By 1820, Gia Long's successor, Minh Mang, could no longer completely prevent the steady encroachment of foreigners upon his land. Instead of welcoming the Europeans and learning what useful knowledge they might possess, Minh Mang created a bureau of interpreters to study Western languages solely for the purpose of preparing Vietnamese replies to foreign countries—nothing more.

When John Crawfurd, a British ambassador in India, arrived in the ancient capital, Hue (pronounced "hway"), in 1828, the emperor again refused to meet a European. Although the French had been making inroads into Vietnam, no European state had been afforded any special privileges in trade. The Nguyen were highly suspicious of foreign motives. "In our new residence we found ourselves treated with perfect respect, but we were close prisoners," Crawfurd noted in his record of the mission. "Interpreters and Cochin Chinese servants were always at hand to do every office for us, but our Indian servants were not allowed to move beyond the doors without two or three persons to watch them, and this only once or twice in the course of the day."[15]

The military power of the European "barbarians" was not lost on the emperor. Recognizing that the foreigners were highly advanced in their war-making capabilities, by 1836 he had begun purchasing English gunpowder, muskets, and even one Western steamship. Then, in 1839, Vietnam constructed a factory to replicate the ship's engine. It was a debacle of no small order. Without Western-trained engineers or blueprints,

Vietnam's efforts at engine manufacturing proved largely futile. Vietnam's leaders were eager to adopt the West's technological prowess, but they wanted to do it without the foreigners, their education, and their modern skills. The Vietnamese strove to avoid a deeper knowledge of the West, perhaps fearing that once Western ways arrived in their land, they would no longer be able to control them.[16]

Western trade representatives soon learned that the sword was mightier than the pen. The Opium Wars began in 1839, when Western naval powers bombarded Chinese ports, demanding the right to sell drugs to Chinese subjects. Within a few short years, the Chinese had no choice but to capitulate, while China's neighbors grew anxious, wondering who would be next. Minh Mang and his regime recognized the Western threat, but they believed that limiting contact was still the wisest course. The question before the emperor was how, and how much, those interactions could plausibly be restricted. A heated debate arose over the issue at the highest levels.

Emperor Minh Mang not only faced the potentially hostile Europeans at the gates of his land, he also confronted a xenophobic adviser within his own court. Vu Duc Khue, a leading scholar-official, insisted that the wisest step for Vietnam was to shun all contact with the Europeans. He attacked Westerners as dangerous barbarians who should be uniformly repelled. He pointed to the Opium Wars as proof of what trading with the Western powers would lead to—humiliation and subjugation. Vu called for a total halt to trade with the Europeans. The only problem with such a plan, Vu conceded, was that it would cut Vietnam off from gaining information about the West.[17]

In response to Vu's challenge, Emperor Minh Mang delivered the longest written reply of his reign. First, the emperor insisted that Vietnam could not survive without foreign trade.

Attempting to do so, he argued, would bankrupt the nation's sugar producers, who depended on export sales. Severing trade ties would also deprive Vietnam of critical war matériel—muskets and gunpowder—as well as textiles. Minh Mang understood that total isolation was neither possible nor beneficial. The question was how to profit from the Europeans without being subjugated by them.

The emperor confronted this dilemma head-on. He argued that the Opium Wars had resulted partly from an unwise Chinese policy of permitting the foreigners to live within their country. This had fostered trade but simultaneously made it impossible to control them. When the barbarians reside in a land, Minh Mang noted, they sketch maps of strategic points. Since Vietnam forced the foreigners to sail away after goods have been exchanged, Vietnam, he insisted, would be safe. The French would prove him wrong.

The Nguyen rulers were tightly bound by the infovoiding cognition trap. While Minh Mang clearly desired the benefits of European trade, manufacturing, and war matériel, he thought he could obtain them without deep knowledge of the Europeans. This was true of the dynasty's leaders as a whole. They were infovoiders, convinced that they could remain sheltered inside an information void and still achieve their objectives: independence, economic growth, and power. In 1847, Tu Duc assumed the throne as the third Nguyen ruler and continued the same foreign policies of his predecessors with respect to Western ideas. The results were disastrous. French warships bombarded Da Nang in 1847, and from the late 1850s onward French forces progressively extended their control over all of Indochina, subjecting its inhabitants to the economic, political, and social upheavals of colonization. Infovoiding was not the sole cause of Vietnam's defeat, but it was a key factor and an error that could have been prevented. In fact, infovoiding was actively rejected by a different Southeast Asian nation not far from Vietnam.

KING MONGKUT'S HAND

Rama II knew he was dying. Just three weeks earlier the royal white elephant had expired. It was an ill omen, and the king understood precisely what it meant. Summoning his closest advisers to his side, Rama II explained who would ascend to the throne upon his death. His son Mongkut had to seem the most rational choice. Born with a keen intellect, curiosity, and an openness to the world beyond the palace, Mongkut could guide Siam (present-day Thailand) wisely in its ever closer dealings with the Western powers. But Rama II sensed what his advisers did not. His son's youth and inexperience might make him susceptible to internal palace intrigues. Perhaps he saw the white elephant's death as a sign of danger for the dynasty if his heir succeeded him too soon. Whatever his motives might have been, when his advisers were at hand, the king declared that Mongkut was ready—not for the throne, but instead for the Buddhist monkhood.

And so, in 1824, Chetsadabodin, a thirty-six-year-old leading figure in Rama II's government and the king's son by a royal concubine, was anointed Rama III, while Mongkut remained safely cloistered among the monks of Bangkok. For nearly the next thirty years, Mongkut turned his mind to an internal journey that would prepare him for leadership better than any of his contemporaries. He would need all the mental training he could manage, because during his kingship Siam would confront the most serious challenge to its freedom.

Thirty years before Mongkut ascended to the throne, his curious, dynamic intellect was already evident. Buddhist monks were meant to meditate. That is how the monks of Siam had always been trained. But Mongkut quickly grew dissatisfied with his traditional instruction in the monastery. Believing that most Siamese mindlessly observed Buddhist rituals without understanding their true intentions, he set about learning Pali, the ancient language of Buddhist scripture, in order to read his religion's teachings in the original. After consuming enough of the ancient Pali texts, Mongkut determined to change the monkhood from within. Through a combination of his imposing dynastic lineage and natural charisma, Mongkut proceeded to reorient the way in which Buddhist monks were taught, overseeing the scholarly training of a generation. In the process, he traveled widely throughout the Siamese kingdom, meeting Siamese from many stations in life. On these journeys, the peculiar monk with a probing nature was able to talk with Siamese about their concerns. He came to know what made his people tick. And in those people he discovered an openness of spirit. It was an education normally never available to a would-be king, and it equipped him with a soundness of judgment that was arguably unparalleled in the region.

Mongkut was not alone in his fascination with and openness to information about the Western world. A number of young Siamese elites were embracing certain aspects of Western ways. Prince Chudamani became proficient in English, and because of his military responsibilities, he equipped and drilled his troops in Western fashion. Prince Wongsathirat, who oversaw the government's division of royal physicians, decided to study Western medicine himself, eventually earning a correspondence diploma from a medical school in Philadelphia. Yet it was Mongkut who possessed a broad, diverse knowledge not only of Western languages and science, but also of Westerners themselves. His fascination with religious life led him to engage the

Protestant and Catholic missionaries living in Bangkok, contacts he maintained over the years to his benefit.[18]

Once Mongkut finally became king, it did not take long before he met the first and possibly gravest test of his reign. In 1855, a British delegation headed by Sir John Bowring, governor of British Hong Kong, arrived to press for a trade agreement. Britain had controlled India since 1756 and later conquered Siam's neighbors Burma and Malaya, the latter with its critical geostrategic port at Singapore. In Burma's case, Britain had used a commercial disagreement as a pretext for war and annexation. Mongkut understood the power imbalance fully. He recognized that if Bowring's mission failed to produce an arrangement acceptable to the British, Siam's freedom might cease.

First impressions matter, and Mongkut spared no effort to impress his honored guest. The king orchestrated a welcoming event down to the last detail. Bowring's mission officially began on April 4, 1855, at a quarter to eight in the evening, when King Mongkut dispatched his own boat to ferry the Englishman across the river to the palace. Bowring was placed in an ornate chair and borne through the streets by eight men. Hundreds of torchbearers guided the way through passageways and open grounds. At each set of gates, royal guards stood at attention, presenting arms in European fashion. Once through the final gate, Bowring entered an inner courtyard. By the moonlight, he saw the king seated upon a magnificent throne, clad in crimson garb and a headdress sparkling with diamonds and precious stones. He wore a golden girdle and a short, jewel-encrusted dagger. Yet instead of making Bowring prostrate himself before his royal highness, as was the custom, Mongkut greeted his guest in English and invited him to sit opposite the king with only a table between them. The king called for liqueurs, teas, and sweetmeats for both to dine on. And then, in a wholly uncustomary, unregal act, King Mongkut offered Bowring some fine cigars from his own hand.

The king's efforts to impress Bowring did not end there. Two days later, the king entertained Bowring in his private quarters. Mongkut's thirst for information about the West was evident even from the decor. The king's living quarters were lined with new books. There were timepieces of all varieties. Thermometers, barometers, and similar meteorological devices stood in full view. Mongkut even possessed statues of Queen Victoria and Prince Albert. Bowring noted in his diary, "Almost everything seemed English."[19]

Within two weeks of their first meeting, an agreement was struck. To celebrate, the king prepared a spectacle with pomp and circumstance to rival any the English crown might provide. Once again, human bearers were sent to carry Bowring and his party to the palace, with thousands of soldiers, courtiers, and onlookers lining the way. Once inside the royal confines, an unbroken line of magisterial personages stood at attention, bedecked in every imaginable costume and dress. They were adorned with spears, swords, shields, bucklers, battle-axes, bows, and quivers. Their colorful costumes ranged, as Bowring put it, from the fierce to the farcical. To Bowring's amazement, some of the highest-ranking nobles stood naked above the waist. The British guests were then ushered into a royal reception hall to await the king's official summons. To make them feel at home, they were seated at a long table replete with fresh water in gold and silver vessels. Servants brought them coffee and cigars.[20] Bowring, seated at the table's head, must have been impressed. Although he had harbored some misgivings during the brief days of negotiation, he must have concluded at least one thing about the Siamese: these were people with whom he could do business.

The Bowring Agreement's terms were extremely favorable to the British. Mongkut granted the principal British demands: a reduction of tariffs to 3 percent, full diplomatic recognition, and extraterritoriality for British subjects. Hardest of all from the king's vantage point, he agreed to abolish all government commodity and trading monopolies. It was from these state-controlled enterprises that the state received its greatest share of income. Countless Siamese had depended on them for their livelihood. But here was yet another of Mongkut's mental gifts: he did not think linearly. He devised an alternative solution by retaining hold of the opium monopoly and introducing new vice taxes on gambling, alcohol, and the lottery. As a result, state revenues only fell during the first year following these changes. Thereafter they returned to their pre–Bowring Agreement levels.

But Mongkut was not done dealing yet. The Bowring Agreement was merely the first in a clever series of diplomatic maneuvers. The king quickly moved to sign similar agreements with France, the United States, and other Western powers, being careful not to permit any one foreign nation exclusive rights in Siam. This enabled him to play each power off against the others in the ongoing battle for a dominant position in trade. And Mongkut went one step further. He also exploited the divergent interests and agendas within nations. Using his knowledge of Western governments, he correctly gleaned that the British Foreign Office was not always pursuing the same ends as its India government or its colonial authority in Malaya. Seizing upon these differing aims, he created situations in which each part of the British colonial organization worked at cross-purposes to the others. This strategy helped him to weaken British control and hinder a unified British policy. He played the same game with France, pitting the foreign ministry (the Quai d'Orsay) against the French colonial administration in Saigon.

The Bowring Agreement signaled an extraordinary victory in the history of colonialism. Though the British wrested very favorable terms from Siam, Mongkut preserved his nation's freedom and set the country on a course for independence, even as the nations around them fell one after the other to European rule. Not one of Thailand's neighbors escaped colonization. The Portuguese, Spanish, Dutch, British, French, and later the Japanese all extended their dominion over parts of Southeast Asia. Only Thailand remained free.

Throughout his reign, Mongkut continued to reform Siamese society, permitting his subjects to petition him with their grievances and peer at his face when he passed by. He modernized the technical apparatus of government, granted women greater freedom in marriage, and launched a state-run gazette publishing the new laws in order that his subjects could be better informed. On October 1, 1868, Mongkut succumbed to malaria, which he and his son had contracted in Malaya after traveling there to witness a solar eclipse, his fascination with astronomy never having waned. Mongkut's son Chulalongkorn was heir not just to his father's throne, but to his father's thirst for information about the wider world. Wanting to ensure that his son received as outward and progressive an education as he himself had enjoyed, Mongkut had recruited a private tutor for Chulalongkorn. Her job was to supplement the prince's traditional education with Western science and culture. Anna Leonowens has since been immortalized in the Rodgers and Hammerstein musical *The King and I* and was more recently portrayed by Jodie Foster in the film *Anna and the King*. Chulalongkorn, who became Rama V, ruled Siam until 1910, by which time the age of European colonization had ended as the European powers began their tortuous descent into two world wars.

Under Mongkut's and Chulalongkorn's leadership, Siam achieved what no other Southeast Asian nation and few other non-European nations ever accomplished. It preserved its freedom, not through war, but through the avoidance of war by skillful exploitation of information.[21] These were extraordinary leaders, not because of their intellects, but because of their openness to information. They were *infominded*: eager to embrace as much knowledge as they could absorb. They did not fear alternative views or foreign customs; they engaged them. Other religions did not threaten their worldviews; they expanded them. Free-flowing discussions with those of differing opinions excited them, stretching their ever active minds. They were what the Germans call *Weltoffen*, open to the world and its rich diversity of ideas. Their infomindedness alone cannot completely explain why Siam escaped colonization, but any explanation must include the leaders' imaginative openness to information.[22]

THE COLD EQUATIONS

I want to ask you a question about money. How much would you guess the top financial manager in America makes per year? Think about it realistically and make your best guesstimate. Ten million? Fifty million? A hundred? In 2005, Jim Simons earned $1.5 billion—that was his personal income in just a single year. In 2006 he did even better. He earned $1.7 billion. It is estimated that in 2007 he brought in more than $2 billion. That figure looks like this: $2,000,000,000.00. For much of the last decade, Jim Simons has managed to earn a staggeringly high

salary year after year, making him one of the highest-paid people in the world. Yet little is known about him by the general
public. This kind of quietness requires substantial control over
information. Not surprisingly, information control is the nature
of Simons's trade.

Unlike Long-Term Capital Management, which flared to
prominence, then went bust in spectacular fashion, Jim Simons's
Renaissance Technologies has been steadily making record
profits for its investors. Its flagship Medallion fund has yielded
an average 38 percent annual return since its inception in 1988.
The fund has lost money only in a single year, 1989, when it
dropped 4.1 percent. In 1993, Simons closed the fund to new
investors. The fortunate few who found it before then are now
enjoying extraordinary returns.

Given its astonishing success rate, Renaissance is arguably the
last company you would associate with the word "blunder." Yet
it's worth considering how a company could sabotage its own
success through infomania. We can benefit by thinking about
potential blunders just as much as we can by studying those that
have already occurred. As Machiavelli once cautioned in *The
Prince*, it is the doom of men that they fail to see a storm on the
horizon when the sea is calm.

Keeping secrets is one of the keys to Simons's success, and
every Renaissance employee must know it. If its formulas for
cracking market patterns were known even to a single rival
hedge fund, the profitability of both companies would de-
crease. Part of what makes Renaissance work is its tight control
over that code, the sequences secured in the minds and mainframes of its creators. For Renaissance to remain king of the
hedge fund mountain, the protectors of its cold equations must
be the tightest-lipped crew on Long Island. If their control of
information should go too far, however, they might make their

own employees reluctant to exchange ideas within the company. The effect could be a drop in their imaginative output. The pitfall is not far-fetched, considering the recent lawsuit they've had to endure. But before I tell you that story, I should first explain how Renaissance came to be the most consistently profitable hedge fund in the world.

Renaissance headquarters did not always look like a Swiss chalet, the way it does today. Before the complex installed its three tennis courts, professional kitchen, and first-class lecture hall, Renaissance's office space had to be modest. But Professor Simons must have had a vision, for the complex and the company. He certainly had a mind for the shape of things to come. After earning a Ph.D. in mathematics at Berkeley, Simons taught briefly at Harvard and MIT before the twenty-three-year-old professor was hired as a code breaker by the Institute for Defense Analyses, a research organization contracted by the Defense Department. In an interview with *Newsweek*, Simons criticized a *New York Times Magazine* article that he felt presented a much too optimistic view of the war in Vietnam. Simons says he was fired as a result.

He next landed a job as chairman of the mathematics department at the State University of New York, Stony Brook. It was there, in 1974, that he published "Characteristic Forms and Geometric Invariants," in which he developed the Chern-Simons Theory, a breakthrough in theoretical geometry that has since been applied to areas of physics from string theory to supergravity to black holes. In 1985, Simons left academia to found Renaissance on a quiet corner of Long Island.

Over the years, Simons has collected some sixty mathematicians, code breakers, and stellar astrophysicists to, in essence, crack the putatively random movements of Wall Street. His hedge fund scholars search for patterns amid the vast expanse of market data. Their mission is to locate inefficiencies and devise ways to exploit them. So far, his scientists have made a mockery of the "random walk" thesis, the idea that market fluctuations are no more predictable than the staggering steps of a drunkard. As of January 2007, the company's Medallion fund alone had a capitalization of $5.3 billion. Renaissance's total capitalization has blossomed from an initially modest sum to approximately $35 billion, ranking among the wealthiest few in the world. Compared to the competition, its returns are among the most consistent and least volatile in the business.[23]

Today Renaissance finds itself facing the curse of all who must protect essential secrets. They could be at risk of crossing the line from safeguarding information to infomisering. Two former employees, Pavel Volfbeyn and Alexander Belopolsky, have founded a hedge fund within Millennium Partners, a competing company, which Renaissance claims is profiting from the trade secrets those employees learned while at Renaissance. The lawsuit has been costly and time consuming. Astonishingly, a company that is built around information control to protect its trade secrets failed to make Volfbeyn and Belopolsky sign noncompete agreements when they were hired. When both employees were promoted to principals at Renaissance, the company again failed to make them sign. Renaissance recognized too late that its employees could take Renaissance's techniques and use them in a separate company to compete against their former boss. Once Renaissance realized the danger, it insisted that Volfbeyn and Belopolsky sign noncompete agreements. When they refused, they were fired.[24]

Infomisering is not the same as protecting sensitive information. It makes sense to guard trade secrets, protect privacy, and compartmentalize intelligence needed for national security. Infomisering comes when guarding information goes too far. It is a question of degree. The obsessive control of information can cause even the best plans to backfire, because it often produces a counterreaction from those who are being denied essential information.

Whether or not Volfbeyn and Belopolsky were stealing Renaissance's trade secrets, the effect of this lawsuit is that Renaissance may need to tighten its control over information even more than before. Potential employees could then be reluctant to join the Renaissance team if they had to agree to terms that would make it virtually impossible for them to earn a living in related fields if they ever left the company. That's of course what Volfbeyn and Belopolsky have claimed. But the case could also lead Renaissance to infomisering within the company, blocking the free flow of information inside its walls. When individuals, businesses, or nations become infomisers and stymie the free flow of essential information, they constrict the imaginative leaps that best occur when knowledge and ideas are widely shared.

For Renaissance, information control has been a source of their success, at least so far. The question is whether the short-term value of control will morph into infomisering and eventually produce a long-term blunder.

INFOMADNESS

Although the two types of infomaniacs—infomisers and infovoiders—manifest their obsession in different ways, they do share certain traits. One key similarity is that both types retreat from the wisdom of others. Infomisers think that keeping information to themselves is the best way to advance their agenda or defend their position. They rarely grasp that their hoarding of data undermines their aims. First, it engenders resentment among their peers, who may therefore try to undercut them, and second, it prevents other capable people from pointing out the weaknesses embedded in their plans. Without thoughtful feedback from well-informed colleagues, most of us are much more likely to go awry. Both Yosuke Matsuoka and Saddam Hussein achieved their short-term aims through infomisering, yet they lost power partly from the same act. Put another way, they won the battle for information but lost the war that truly mattered. Had they allowed a free flow of information, their colleagues could have saved them from themselves.

The same holds true for infovoiders. Decision makers who turn away from the knowledge of others usually weaken themselves. Bishop de Landa sabotaged his mission to convert the Mayans by destroying priceless information about his subjects. The Vietnamese emperors thwarted their hope of preserving their independence by rejecting knowledge about the Europeans, even as the Europeans offered ample opportunities to be observed. Infovoiders do not typically try to limit their knowledge for fear of information overload. They blunder precisely because they do not grasp that the quantity of information is not the problem.

Some people believe that too much information is a dangerous thing, but it is only this idea that is dangerous. As the Vietnamese emperors belatedly discovered, too little information weakened their position. The Siamese under kings Mongkut and Chulalongkorn, in contrast, consumed enormous amounts of information about the Europeans, and this vast quantity of knowledge helped Siam to preserve its freedom. If the Siamese had possessed only a thin slice of information about the Europeans, their decision-making process could not have been as prudent, nor their solutions as wise. They needed a tremendous amount of data on European customs, history, intentions, and culture in order to defend against them. The notion that too much information can be a distraction is off the mark. The quantity of information is irrelevant; it is the relevance of any quantity that matters.

Chapter 6

MIRROR IMAGING

Thinking the Other Side Thinks Like Us

PIG THINK

The cows simply would not budge, and no one could figure out why. They were supposed to march placidly into the slaughterhouse as they always had, but the cattle would only approach the door and go no farther. It almost seemed like an act of organized resistance.

The plant owners tried everything, but not even electric cattle prods would get those cows through the door. Having exhausted every plausible explanation, the owners were about to tear down the plant completely and rebuild it from the ground up—at considerable cost in time and profits. But before they committed themselves to such an expensive solution, they made one final effort, placing a call to an unusual livestock expert.

Enter Temple Grandin. Grandin, a professor of animal science at Colorado State University, is autistic. Her condition and her expertise made her reputation so widespread that when Dustin Hoffman was researching his role as the autistic older brother in *Rain Man*, he went to see her for advice on how to play the part. Grandin believes that her autism gives her special insight into how animals think, and in the case of the rebellious cows, that turned out to be true.

Grandin explains that what many animal handlers fail to do is see things from the animal's perspective. They don't realize that animals are what she calls "hyper-specific," drawn to minute details. The subtlest changes in the environment, in light, sound, smell, or texture, can easily upset them, not unlike autistic people. The changes seem subtle to humans, but not to animals. It could be a jiggling chain, the reflection from a tiny puddle, or the hum from an overhead fan that sets them off. In this case, Grandin saw the problem immediately. The entrance to the slaughterhouse was extremely dark. Humans are used to the dilation of our pupils when we move from a bright to a dark space, and this sudden momentary adjustment in vision is not distressing. But to cattle it is a deeply upsetting experience. Grandin's solution was simple: Open the barn's sliding side door to let in more light. As soon as they did, the cows went marching in.

The people operating this slaughterhouse were on the brink of wasting enormous sums and undercutting their own business, all because they fell prey to mirror imaging. Mirror imaging is the cognition trap in which we assume, consciously or unconsciously, that the other side will think and act like us. It is arguably the most prevalent cognition trap around because we all tend to ignore those things that are not important to us. We have an almost instinctive difficulty imagining how others might perceive things differently from the way we ourselves perceive them. "I always tell people, whenever you're having a problem with an animal, try to see what the animal is seeing and experience what the animal is experiencing," Grandin writes. "At that feed lot, all they needed to do was get more light inside the barn. They could have fixed the problem themselves in five minutes if they'd been able to think about the chute from the animal's point of view."

Grandin's genius at understanding the animal mind is extraordinary and rare, yet even she has been guilty of mirror imaging. She tells the story of an alpha sow, the dominant pig in a pen, who repeatedly challenged Grandin's dominant position as the human. The sow behaved aggressively toward Grandin each time she entered the pen. Grandin tried shouting at the pig, which had no effect at all. She tried slapping the sow on the butt to make her obey. This, too, did nothing.

It wasn't until Grandin remembered that she had to put herself in the mind of a dominant pig that the answer became clear. Pigs establish a dominance hierarchy by biting each other on the neck. The strongest pig then pushes all the others down or against the fence. So Grandin took a long wooden plank with a sharp edge and pressed it against the sow's neck. She kept on pressing until she pinned the sow against the fence, and then she let her go. From that moment on, Grandin was boss. This particular dominant sow weighed one hundred pounds, but even a hefty pig is no match for a grown human with a sharp stick. Grandin didn't hurt the pig and didn't need to. She just needed to demonstrate her superiority in a way that a pig could understand. In the language of cognition traps, she had to remember that the other side doesn't always think like us. In this case, she just had to think like a pig.

You might expect that getting ourselves into the minds of other people would be easier than thinking like an animal. In fact, it may actually be even harder, especially when gender differences separate us. Much of male-female relationships involve an almost constant struggle to see situations and interpret comments from the other person's point of view. The linguist Deborah Tannen tells the story of a woman named Eve who had a lump removed from her breast. When she told her female friends how unhappy she was with the appearance of a postoperative scar, her friends all empathized and shared similar complaints.

But when Eve told her husband about her feelings, he responded that she could always have plastic surgery to remove the scar. Eve was hurt, interpreting her husband's words to mean that he thought she looked unattractive and that he wanted her to have more surgery after she had just told him how difficult the first operation had been. Her husband was stunned by her reaction. He was only trying to be sympathetic and offer a solution to comfort her. He told her he didn't care about the scar and thought she looked fine.[1] Eve angrily declared that she would not have any more surgery. She wanted validation of her feelings; her husband thought she wanted what he would have wanted: a solution.

Of course, it is just as hard for women to grasp what men are thinking. Tannen relates another typical scene of a woman who had her boyfriend spend the night with her for the first time. The next morning he suggested that they both go in late to work and eat breakfast together. She was thrilled. It seemed like a wonderfully romantic suggestion. But as soon as she had brought out a beautiful and lovingly prepared meal, he put up his newspaper and began to read. This was not exactly the romantic scene she had been hoping for. In fact, this type of scene had played out many times before. This time, however, she was able to break free from mirror imaging. Having learned more about how men think, she understood that her boyfriend saw this time together as a relief from the burden of having to speak and impress others, the kind of burden he often felt at work. For him, this moment signaled his ease in her presence, a time he could just relax and be at peace in her company. To him, it was very intimate. Recognizing this, she didn't feel compelled to boot him out the door. She knew she might bring him to the point where he also understood that the intimacy she desired came through conversation, not silence.

John Gray's *Men Are from Mars, Women Are from Venus* has sold more than thirty million copies, been translated into forty languages, and in 2004 was rereleased, twelve years after its first printing. His observations clearly struck a chord in the ongoing effort for intergender understanding, a chord that seems to resonate almost universally. His book, of course, is a study in mirror imaging. In example after example within those pages, couples are shown to be confused by the opposite gender's actions. The reason, Gray suggests, is clear. Each sex projects its own expectations onto the other. "We mistakenly assume that if our partners love us, they will react and behave in certain ways: the ways we react and behave when we love someone. This attitude sets us up to be disappointed, again and again." Gray argues that heterosexual relationships are riven by conflict because each sex fails to understand how the other thinks. "Men mistakenly expect women to think, communicate, and act the way men do. Women mistakenly expect men to feel, communicate, and respond the way women do. We have forgotten that men and women are supposed to be different."[2]

Gray's book is merely the most famous example from a large body of literature designed to help break the mirror imaging cognition trap. The fact that so many relationships experience these kinds of misunderstandings is evidence of the powerful spell that mirror imaging casts on us all. As challenging as it is to overcome between the sexes, it can be even harder when facing other cultures during war and peace. And this is true in dealing with enemies and allies alike.

THE PATRIOTIC PROSTITUTES

Most governments, whether at the local or the national level, are usually uneasy about sanctioning prostitution. Neighborhood communities don't want it in their backyards, and federal politicians win few votes by calling for legalizing the oldest profession. But in postwar Japan, the government not only legalized the activity, it actually promoted it.

The Japanese government euphemistically dubbed them "Recreation and Amusement Associations," but soldiers knew what that meant. Scores of these brothels were erected across Japan immediately after the war to service the flood of American GIs arriving to occupy the conquered nation. The women volunteered for many reasons, primary among them being hunger. Postwar Japan was decimated. Food was scarce and living conditions grim. Women who were surviving on a rice ball per day came in hope of just earning enough to survive. Others came in curiosity, unaware of exactly what they would be asked to do. Behind the government-sponsored recruitment drive rested a simple message. Japanese women have a patriotic duty to fulfill, and now is the time for good young women to come to the aid of their country.

For fifteen yen—less than a pack of cigarettes—an American soldier could enjoy a Japanese prostitute for an hour. For not much more he could have her services for the entire night. To help the brothels function unencumbered, authorities established designated zones for them within cities. The entire operation was conducted at the Japanese government's initiative.

The proud men of Japan decided it was necessary to organize their young women into bands of brothels partly out of mirror imaging. The Pacific War had not just been bloody; it had been brutal. The rape of Nanjing symbolized the cruelty of the entire Pacific conflict. Japanese soldiers had engaged in a protracted mass rape of Chinese women while they occupied parts of that country. After the war and the two atomic bombs, the Japanese government understood, or believed it understood, how an occupying force treats the defeated nation's women. They had every reason to assume that the American soldiers would behave exactly as the Japanese had done, or possibly worse. The RAA centers were intended to spare the majority of Japanese women, and their husbands, fathers, and sons, the indignity of being raped. By making prostitutes readily available to the Americans, the Japanese government believed it could preserve the national honor.

What actually occurred, of course, was an upsurge in prostitution and the costs that typically ensue. Young women served an average of fifteen to sixty GIs per day. For some, the demands were too great, and many suffered breakdowns or deserted. One nineteen-year-old simply could not bear her new circumstances and soon after beginning the job took her own life. But the RAA centers proved popular among GIs and soon expanded beyond Tokyo to twenty other cities. As the centers spread, so did venereal disease. Ninety percent of RAA women tested positive for sexually transmitted diseases. Large portions of U.S. troops suffered as well, with one unit testing as high as 70 percent for syphilis and 50 percent for gonorrhea. Concerned by the rising epidemic of venereal disease, in January 1946 the Allied occupation forces banned the RAA centers, publicly declaring them a violation of women's human rights.[3]

What would have happened if the RAA centers had never been created? Would the American GIs have engaged in the kind of frenzied mass rape that the Japanese soldiers in Nanjing and the Soviet soldiers in East Germany had committed?[4] In both instances the German and Chinese women suffered ongoing abuses, from gang rapes to savage beatings and mutilations. Of course, we can never know for certain exactly what would have been. History is an unforgiving laboratory. Its experiments can be run only once, and never again under precisely the same conditions. But based on the experience of American forces in West Germany, we can at least conjecture that the incidence of rape would have been substantially lower than what the Japanese had inflicted on the Chinese. Inside the American-controlled sector of western Germany, rapes did occur, but in much smaller numbers than in the Soviet eastern zone. However, the rate of prostitution in the American sector was higher than in the Soviet zone. So it is possible that the American forces preferred a commercial transaction for sex over the more violent alternative. If the Japanese government had not sponsored the RAA centers, brothels would have sprung up on their own in response to a market need. But if prostitution had not been legalized and sanctioned, if it had remained part of the black market underground, the more limited access or the shame factor might have made the overall incidence of prostitution significantly lower. In other words, by attempting to preserve the honor of most Japanese women, the government may have inadvertently caused more women to lose their honor than was necessary.

It was difficult for the postwar Japanese leaders to imagine that the Americans would behave any differently from the way the Japanese military had acted in China. The Japanese had demonized the Americans during the war. Since the Americans had firebombed Tokyo and detonated two atomic bombs over their country, destroying two major cities and killing hundreds of thousands in the process, American barbarity probably seemed a reasonable assumption. It was, however, only an assumption. Once the GIs became occupiers, they behaved in a far less brutal fashion than Japanese leaders expected. Had the Japanese understood their enemy better, they could have reduced the rate of prostitution by forcing the practice underground. Failure to know one's enemy, of course, is what drives so many conflicts in war as well as peace.

THE UNEXPECTED ARMY

Colonel Christian Marie Ferdinand de la Croix de Castries seemed the perfect man for the mission. With his striking red cap and scarf, his omnipresent riding crop, and the heavy knotted cane he used to support himself, de Castries combined courage and class with overpowering panache. And in the remote valley of Vietnam's northwest province, French soldiers would need an inspiring leader to bolster morale just in case anything should go wrong, though there seemed little chance of that, especially under de Castries's command.

After the ejection of Japanese forces from Vietnam at the close of World War II, French troops struggled to reestablish control over their colony. Before long, northern Vietnamese forces began battling the French in a quest for national independence. The war dragged on until it reached a crucial juncture in 1953. Establishing a fortress at Dien Bien Phu, the French military intended to turn the war at last in their favor. They devised what seemed like a foolproof plan and chose an incomparable colonel to lead the way.

Even among his aristocratic peers, de Castries stood apart. His lineage was pure military, his ancestors having served France since the Crusades, but his personal traits made him the toast of Parisian high society throughout the 1930s. An accomplished pilot and world champion equestrian, de Castries's daring also made him a relentless gambler burdened by debt. That same élan, combined with his imperial good looks, brought him countless female admirers. His amorous dalliances with the wives of fellow soldiers were near legendary throughout the officer corps, almost as legendary as his courage. In June 1940, operating behind German lines, de Castries and sixty men fought for three days against an entire German battalion. He was taken only after his ammunition, not his spirit, was spent. Then, in a brazen escape, de Castries dug out from a maximum-security camp deep in Poland, made his way across enemy territory to Spain, and joined up with the Free French fighters in Africa, ultimately confronting the Nazis again in the war's final campaigns. In 1946 de Castries led troops in Indochina, and in 1951 he rose to the rank of lieutenant colonel, but then his legs were severely fractured during an ambush. Despite the pain, he managed to compete in horseback riding events that November.[5] In 1953, when de Castries parachuted into Dien Bien Phu, his reputation preceded him. Few others seemed as fit to lead French forces in the most decisive battle of the Indochina War. Unfortunately for France, the attack did not unfold as planned.

The French fortress was supposed to be supremely secure. Instead, the enemy somehow managed to let loose a hellstorm of firepower upon the encampment. As the Vietminh's withering assault continued for an excruciating fifty-six days and nights, de Castries suffered a total mental collapse. He retreated into a shell inside himself and ceased to command altogether. Colonel Keller, chief of de Castries's general staff, suffered a nervous breakdown and had to be relieved of command. The one-armed colonel Charles Piroth, said to be the best artillery commander in the French army, cracked under the relentless Vietminh barrage. Unable to quell the enemy's fire, he retired to his tent and committed suicide. Hundreds of soldiers simply deserted into the hills or were stripped of their rank and made coolies. When the French finally surrendered, defeat was total. More than fifteen hundred French soldiers were dead and more than four thousand had been wounded. The Vietminh took thousands of French troops prisoner and marched them for miles through the jungle. Hundreds died along the way. Those who survived the march endured malaria and malnutrition. The Geneva Accords of 1954 produced a complete French withdrawal from Vietnam and the division of the country into two states. Dien Bien Phu marked the nadir of French power since its defeat by Nazi Germany in 1940. From that loss in northern Vietnam forward, its once mighty colonial empire would disintegrate.[6]

What happened to France at Dien Bien Phu? How did a technologically advanced nation, with firepower superior to that of the Vietminh, manage to lose so badly in the war's most pivotal campaign? In similar set-piece battles earlier in the war, French forces had routed Vietminh troops handily. Dien Bien Phu, a valley in the northwest of Vietnam surrounded by nearly impassable hills and daunting terrain, seemed in every way to favor the French. Backed by the able French air force, soldiers could be readily supplied by air drops. Reinforcements could even be parachuted in if necessary. More than this, French bombers could sever Vietminh supply lines, destroying the roads and bridges leading to Dien Bien Phu. Without the ability to transport artillery, the Vietminh would be decisively outgunned. For this reason, French military planners had specifically selected Dien Bien Phu as their first choice of sites at which to engage the enemy. Colonel Piroth was so confident of victory that he summed up his battle plan as follows. "Firstly, the Vietminh won't succeed in getting their artillery through to here. Secondly, if they do get here, we'll smash them. Thirdly, even if they manage to keep on shooting, they will be unable to supply their pieces with enough ammunition to do us any real harm."[7] On paper, it looked like the French could not lose. There was only one critical flaw in the plan.

French planners were afflicted with mirror imaging. The French tacticians assumed that the Vietminh would fight the way the French fight, by transporting heavy artillery to a battle-field. The only way the French could transport their supplies through the jungles of Vietnam was by mechanized vehicles—trucks, cars, or airdrops from planes. Since the Vietminh lacked an air force, they would have to use trucks and cars, and without roads and bridges, their heavy weapons could never get through. But what the French planners never counted on was that the Vietminh would not need vehicles. Instead, they relied on Vietnamese villagers, an astonishing two hundred thousand of them.

Rallying the villagers to assist them against the colonial oppressors, the Vietminh organized an unexpected army of peasants to form human chains across the jungle. Women bore bullets wrapped in bags and hung from poles across their backs. Children peddled bicycles laden with baskets of machine parts along roads impassable by cars. The best swimmers crossed rivers back and forth, handing off sacks of supplies to men waiting across the banks. Climbers scaled jagged mountain cliffs to get their cargo through to the next link in the chain. Scores of men pushed backbreakingly heavy artillery pieces up dizzyingly steep hills. Thousands upon thousands of locals marched weapons, munitions, and machine parts through dense jungles. Four thousand six hundred twenty tons of petrol products, 1,360 tons of ammunition, 46 tons of spare weapons, and 2,260 tons of consumable goods, including 1,700 tons of rice, sustained the thousands of Vietminh soldiers at Dien Bien Phu. In all, some 8,286 tons of supplies were transported more than 600 miles from China to the battle site. Among those supplies were the antiaircraft guns, which effectively starved the French garrison of reinforcements, matériel, and food.[8] The entire operation epitomized Vietnamese resourcefulness. It demonstrated the Vietminh leadership's mastery of logistics. It underscored the Vietminh's attractiveness as an alternative to the French. But more than anything else, Dien Bien Phu showed how badly French planners had failed to see the danger of cognition traps.

At Dien Bien Phu, mirror imaging led the French to overlook the capacity of the Vietminh leadership to find low-tech solutions. Where the French thought machine transport was essential, the Vietnamese found that their feet, hands, and backs could do the job instead. French forces in Vietnam could not have carried out such a low-tech solution, not just because they lacked the numbers of human bodies to support them, but also because they did not think like the Vietminh did. As a result, the Vietminh's innovation never occurred to French planners.

Unlike the French military leaders, President Dwight Eisenhower managed to see the conflict as the Vietminh and their supporters saw it. Eisenhower avoided committing American air power or ground troops to Dien Bien Phu, despite France's desperate pleas for assistance. Nearly all his civilian advisers, including Vice President Richard Nixon, argued vehemently for America to intervene, but Eisenhower overruled them all. His wisdom stemmed from more than mere intuition. It came in part from his ability to imagine how many Vietnamese would perceive American intervention.

President Eisenhower was barely into the second year of his first term when the French crisis crashed at his door. As the fate of Colonel de Castries and his men looked increasingly bleak, France called on America for help. Anxious to gain U.S. air support that could rescue the embattled French garrison under siege, French foreign minister Georges Bidault met with American ambassador Douglas Dillon in Paris on April 4. Employing the starkest terms he could, Bidault stated simply, "For good or evil, the fate of Southeast Asia now rest[s] on Dien Bien Phu."[9]

Eisenhower had been elected on a pledge of "No more Chinas, no more Koreas." After China fell to communism during President Truman's watch, all subsequent presidents feared being tainted with the charge of having lost territory to Soviet influence. Throughout protracted, heated debates, Eisenhower's inner circle demanded the use of U.S. force to stop Ho Chi Minh from winning at Dien Bien Phu, but Eisenhower would have none of it, partly because intervention found little support. Despite Secretary of State Dulles's best efforts, no U.S. allies could be convinced to intervene in the rescue of besieged French forces. "The concept of leadership implied associates," Ike insisted. "Without them, the leader is just an adventurer like Genghis Khan."[10]

The president possessed grave doubts about intervention even as early as 1951. He wrote in his diary that he was convinced that no military victory was possible in the Indochina theater.[11] By 1954, Eisenhower's military advisers were counseling against committing troops to Vietnam. General Matthew Ridgway informed the president that effective intervention would require ten divisions and the casualties would be high. In spite of these realities, the president's key civilian advisers countered that America needed to block communism at all points, wherever it threatened freedom. Recognizing this was more than simply a Soviet-led drive for expansion, Eisenhower disagreed. He grasped the perspective of many Vietnamese that they were fighting for their freedom. He declared, "The cause of the free world could never win, the United States could never survive, if we frittered away our resources in local engagements."[12]

Why was Eisenhower snared by the flatview cognition trap over Iran, yet able to escape mirror imaging over Dien Bien Phu one year later? After all, Eisenhower shared much of the

Cold War's flatview, whereby conflicts often seemed colored by communist hues. Given this view, Iran, Guatemala, Cuba, and other covert American interventions seemed justified. But covertly overthrowing a foreign leader is a distinctly different matter from overtly committing American soldiers to a foreign war. On one level, Eisenhower knew that military ventures in far-off lands are best undertaken with the robust aid of true allies. From firsthand experience working intimately with the Allied commanders of World War II, General Eisenhower appreciated the value of true multinational coalitions. His particular military experience afforded him a broader perspective than that of his successors, but there was more to Ike's decision against war than pure military calculations.

Unlike his advisers, the president escaped mirror imaging over Dien Bien Phu by exhibiting a degree of empathy with the Vietnamese people. In 1954, he had the sensitivity to see in Vietnam a people's struggle for independence intertwined with communist aspirations. "If the French indeed collapsed and the United States moved in," he told his National Security Council, "we would in the eyes of many Asiatic peoples merely replace French colonialism with American colonialism."[13] At least in this instance, Ike appears to have gauged the anticolonial winds of change sweeping across the postwar developing world. That sensitivity to the specificity of Vietnam's case, his empathy with the struggle against oppression, enabled him to recognize that committing U.S. forces to Vietnam would make America the target of the Vietnamese struggle for national independence, and the United States would be dragged into a quagmire from which it would not readily emerge.

Eisenhower avoided blundering into Vietnam in 1954 not because of his in-depth knowledge of Vietnam's history, language, culture, or people, all of which he lacked. Instead, Ike was not trapped by mirror imaging. *General* Eisenhower saw the military dangers of intervention, and *President* Eisenhower perceived the problems that made Vietnam's struggle distinct. Though he never met Ho Chi Minh or the Vietnamese peasants who supported him, he sensed that the people behind the battle at Dien Bien Phu were too gray to be fitted neatly upon the black-and-white chessboard of Cold War geopolitics. By refusing to categorize Dien Bien Phu as simply one more Cold War clash, Ike resisted a seductive cognition trap. One of the great disappointing aspects of his presidency is that by 1956, his administration's policies shifted. Although he never committed U.S. ground troops to Vietnam, Eisenhower did set America on the course that led his successors, presidents Kennedy and Johnson, to blunder into war.

BUILDING BRIDGES, MISSING POINTS

In 1965, a young second lieutenant named Jeffrey Race completed his bachelor's degree in government at Harvard and set out for Vietnam. It was the first year of America's decade-long commitment of ground troops to that conflict, and Race was full of assumptions about the war, few of which turned out to be correct. But unlike the many thousands of American soldiers who witnessed the failures of U.S. strategy in Vietnam, Race decided to investigate what was going wrong, not after the fact, but while American involvement was just beginning. Race continued on a second tour of duty, serving as a military adviser to the South Vietnamese authorities in Long An province, the region of Vietnam just north of Saigon.

With his army service completed, Race entered Harvard's doctoral program in political science, but he immediately returned to Long An to conduct his dissertation research in 1968–69. He set out by asking a very different question from what others asked, then and since. While others pondered what America was doing wrong, Race asked what the North Vietnamese were doing right. He wanted to understand why the North was so successful at winning hearts and minds. Using his fluency in written and spoken Vietnamese, he interviewed captured North Vietnamese prisoners and studied the North's propaganda. The conclusions he reached revealed a complex, multifaceted explanation, not a one-dimensional easy answer. That said, many of his findings could be placed within a broader observation. The North Vietnamese were extremely sensitive to local grievances, while the South Vietnamese Army and the United States were not. The Americans in particular were engaged in mirror imaging.

Most thoughtful military and political leaders at the time understood the critical importance of winning over local support. The question was how to do it. Race pointed out that most of the American initiatives involved infrastructure efforts: building roads, bridges, hospitals, and elementary schools. In addition, the U.S. tried to spread Western-style medical care: immunizations of children, drug treatments, and the type of health services familiar to Americans. In other words, the U.S. thought that the Vietnamese would be grateful to have those things that Americans have. By building physical bridges, they would be erecting cultural bridges. The problem was not that the Vietnamese did not desire these trappings of modernity; the problem was that they were not their primary concerns.

The North Vietnamese communist forces, in sharp contrast, put themselves in the minds of local villagers. They figured out what Vietnamese villagers really wanted: local justice. Rather than wishing to be catapulted into modernity, many Vietnamese wanted more equitable land distribution, tax policies, and opportunities for upward social mobility. The communists geared their propaganda accordingly. The communists promised fairer land ownership, opposing the system created by the French under colonial rule. They offered fairer taxation, unlike the flat tax imposed since the French rule. And they allowed anyone, regardless of social status, to gain an education and advance within the party administration. This freedom differed dramatically from the South's system, in which mainly the wealthier middle class was educated in French-style schools and granted positions of prominence, such as in the police, military, and other professions. Roads and bridges were good to have, but local justice held much greater appeal.

In 1972, Race published his findings and was promptly ignored. Part of the reason was that his message sounded defeatist. One of his work's implications was that the U.S. had essentially lost the war by the time it had committed ground troops. The communists had more to offer Vietnamese villagers than America even knew how to propose. American leaders were not yet ready for this message.

The same cognition trap that caught the French at Dien Bien Phu just as easily ensnared the Americans ten years later. For the French, mirror imaging foiled their best-laid military plans. For the Americans, it sabotaged their political plans. In both cases, the outsiders thought that the Vietnamese would think and act like the French and Americans. And in both cases their best-laid plans went painfully awry. More recently, mirror imaging has seized some Americans in another conflict, one where building bridges is proving tougher than planned.

Ghost Wars

Hyder Akbar was just nineteen years old in 2003, when he traveled to Afghanistan for the first time. Hyder's father, Fazal, an Afghan-American living with his family in San Francisco, had been called by his old friend, Hamid Karzai, now the newly appointed president of Afghanistan. Karzai asked Hyder's father to serve as governor of Kunar province, a region along the Pakistani border. Hyder wanted to go along.

Although post-Taliban Afghanistan was dangerous, Hyder quickly found he had a useful role for the American forces operating in Kunar. Hyder was fluent in Pashto, the local language, and he could serve as a translator. Hyder did something more than just translate, though. He kept an extensive audio diary of his experiences in Afghanistan, creating a rare listening post for interested outsiders.[14]

Because Hyder possessed greater familiarity with Afghan culture and history than the American soldiers he was assisting, he was able to observe some of the errors the soldiers made in their dealings with Afghans. In his recordings you can hear him translating what the officers and local Afghans are saying to each other, but he later added his own voice-over, in which he explains what, from his perspective, is going wrong.

In one instance, an American officer has arrived in a section of Kunar to help resolve a dispute. Many of the locals are refusing to pay taxes to the appointed Afghan official, Shah Wali. After the dispute turned violent, the Americans were called in. In a meeting with the feuding factions, the American officer tries to explain to the local Afghans how to behave. His thinking reflects classic mirror imaging: "In the United States, if I get fined by a policeman for driving too fast, but I think I was driving the speed limit, I don't shoot the policeman. I don't run him over and say, 'I'm not going to listen to you because I was right and you were wrong.' I go through the official system."

In the background, you can hear Hyder translating the American officer's words into Pashto, and in the foreground he inserted a voice-over. Here is what Hyder thinks about the conversation.

"This policeman analogy, if you really want to use it, would go something like this: Imagine that this policeman had come into your house and had robbed you like a year ago. And maybe killed a kid or two for you, and just walked outta your house. And then you started fighting him for like six months. And then like the ninth month he comes and gives you a speeding ticket for going fifty-seven in a fifty-five-mile-an-hour zone. That would be more of an accurate analogy about what happened."

As with many foreign interventions, when Americans descended on Afghanistan, they knew little about its history or culture. This particular American officer cannot be blamed for mirror imaging. He had probably never been given the background knowledge he needed for dealing with these kinds of issues. He likely did not know that Shah Wali was a former communist, that the locals who despised him were former mujahideen who lost friends and loved ones battling the communists for years, that the local grievances and sense of injustice between these two factions was intense and long-standing, or that this particular official, Shah Wali, was notorious for his corruption and thuggery. These are the ghosts that haunt so many conflicts where wars have lasted for decades or longer. In societies that are not as mobile as the United States, where families remain rooted in towns and villages for generations, memories are long and enmities run deep. It is not the officer's fault for not knowing all this. It is the U.S. government's responsibility to educate its soldiers and diplomats for more effective communication and negotiations, a responsibility that has too often been overlooked.

BREAKING THE MIRROR

It takes a good deal of empathy to break the mirror of mirror imaging and sense what others are thinking and feeling. And it takes an imaginative leap to envision how a stranger's circumstances might affect his actions. Though the French and Americans failed in Vietnam for multiple and varied reasons, in certain critical respects they both lacked the imagination to think like the Vietminh. Eisenhower escaped mirror imaging in part because he found the empathy and imagination to see the Americans as many Vietnamese might see them. Because he could, his judgment was sound.

Like Eisenhower, President Kennedy also had a powerful moment of cracking the mirror imaging trap. His came during the intense thirteen days of the Cuban Missile Crisis. At one point in the crisis, the air force presented the president with photographs gained from aerial reconnaissance over Cuba. These snapshots showed that Cuban planes were positioned along their airfields wingtip-to-wingtip. The implication was plain. The enemy's fighter jets were sitting ducks. It would require merely a few bombs to wipe out the bulk of their air force. In a move that must have infuriated his generals, JFK refused to order the strike. The president believed that a naval blockade of the island had to be given a chance to work. He wanted to see if the Soviets would back down. A U.S. attack on Cuba might have demanded an equally aggressive response from the Soviets, so any such moves had to be avoided.

Then, in a masterstroke of reverse mirror imaging, Kennedy instructed the air force to run the same reconnaissance flights over American airfields in Florida. JFK was stepping out of his own preconceptions. He was, in essence, trying to see the United States from an enemy's point of view. Once the reconnaissance was complete, an embarrassed air force commander had to report that U.S. fighter jets were also positioned wingtip-to-wingtip— sitting every bit as vulnerable as the Cuban planes. The president immediately ordered the American jets to be repositioned. JFK allegedly remarked to a close colleague, "I guess this is the week I earn my salary."[15] I don't know if the president read poetry, but at the very least he seems to have taken to heart the lesson from the classic eighteenth-century Robert Burns poem "To a Louse":

> O would some Power the gift to give us
> To see ourselves as others see us!
> It would from many a blunder free us . . .

Chapter 7

STATIC CLING

Refusal to Accept a Changing World

THE HIGHLANDS OF New Guinea are a forbidding place. Densely covered in jungles and swamps, and infested on the coasts by malarial mosquitoes, its rugged interior remained unexplored by Europeans for centuries after its discovery. But in 1930, Michael Leahy, a young Australian prospector, ventured inland in search of gold. On his first evening in the Bismarck Mountains, he looked down into the cultivated valley below and gaped wide-eyed in disbelief. New Guinea's Highlands were thought to be uninhabited, but as night fell he saw a landscape glistening with hundreds of tiny, controlled fires. Michael "Mic" Leahy had just stumbled upon one of the last people on earth still living in the Stone Age, untouched by the outside world. In all, there were nearly one million Highlanders who had never seen a wheel, much less a gun. This gap in knowledge gave Leahy an incredible advantage over the natives, and he used it to the fullest.

While this contact was traumatic for the Highlanders, the experience also altered Leahy, more than he realized at the time. The tribes he encountered were startlingly primitive, and Leahy could never envision them as anything else. He could not imagine that they could ever adapt to modern influences and one day govern themselves. To Michael Leahy, the High-landers were just a Stone Age people, and in his mind that is how they would remain. Primitive people, he believed, understand only force.

Static cling is the cognition trap that prevents us from either recognizing or accepting a changing world. It blindsides our imagination just when a broader view is most essential. In static cling, people cannot accept that their surroundings are in fundamental flux. Instead of soberly assessing those changes and adapting to them, those with static cling resist. Their longing for things to remain as they have always been keeps them from prosperity, peace, and success. In Leahy's case, because he could not see that mainstream attitudes toward native peoples were changing, he undermined his search for gold.

In his published account of the New Guinea exploration, *The Land That Time Forgot*, Michael Leahy sanitized the killings. He tells how he and his team typically fired over the Highlanders' heads to frighten them off. When necessary, they shot at their legs. Only in desperation would they actually shoot the men dead. His diary entries, however, reveal a more brutal truth. On November 20, 1932, Leahy wrote: "Wiped off a few Nigs who pinched an axe, and then got too confident and opened up on us." Daniel Leahy's own account decades later also contradicts his older brother's more palatable, published version. "One thing we would never do was to use the rifle to frighten them. The only time we fired the rifle, the battle was absolutely on . . . If someone did get hit, it was meant."

Because the Highlanders had no knowledge of the outside world, they naturally behaved in ways that heightened their primitiveness to Leahy. Assuming that their possessions held supernatural powers, the Highlanders gathered the white people's discarded matchsticks and ate them. They dug up the Leahys' used toilet paper and excrement to burn with pig's blood, holding their hands over the rising smoke in hope it would give them superior strength against their neighbors. Some of the Highlanders believed that the Leahys and the other men in their team were the spirits of their dead relatives. As a result, many were fearful of the white men's supernatural existence and joyful at their return from the dead. Often they identified Mick and other whites, as well as the native New Guinean carriers in his team, as parents, uncles, or children lost in battles. One mother clutched at one of Leahy's carriers, refusing to let him go, convinced he was the son she had lost in war. Although these views helped protect Leahy, he still found it necessary to demonstrate his strength.

As Mick and his team departed a village one morning, two angry-looking natives blocked their path. The Leahys could have fired in the air to frighten them. If rushed, they could have fired at their feet. Instead, Mick and Dan shot them dead. A few days later, Mick again felt threatened. As he noted in his diary, "Had to bump a couple off to show we mean business if they so much as appear to be hostile." Soon after, he wrote, "I think that yesterday's shooting made them realize that we can kill at a distance, and are prepared to keep on killing until they get enough bloody sense to realize that their lives count as nothing compared to the lives of the natives who place their services and lives in our keeping by accompanying us and carrying our cargo." To be sure the Highlanders understood, Leahy left one of their corpses to "decorate" the entrance to his camp.

By 1935, news of the killings had reached London when Michael Leahy himself took his case to the Royal Geographic Society. Leahy was intent on being credited with discovering the New Guinean interior, as another explorer was attempting to claim the discoveries as his own. Although Leahy won his case, in the process he committed an astonishing faux pas. As proof that he was out of touch with prevailing sentiments, he openly described his bloodiest exploits. It simply never struck him that anything was wrong with what he'd done. The tales of his killings appalled some segments of the public. As news of those crimes spread across Europe and North America, groups such as the Anti-Slavery Movement called for tighter restrictions on exploration. Leahy was seen by some as a dangerous rogue adventurer. After two Catholic missionaries were murdered by Highlanders, the Australian administration responded by forbidding further penetration into the interior. Michael Leahy would henceforth be confined to a limited swath of the Highlands, and for the next twenty years, that part of New Guinea would again be closed off to the outside world.

Had Michael Leahy been permitted to continue his exploration, he probably would have become a wealthy man. Years later, one of Mick Leahy's rivals hit the jackpot when he struck gold beyond the area where the Leahys had once explored. Mick Leahy, who never found his own river of gold, had to endure the indignity of Australia's retreat from colonial rule. Decades later, as calls for self-determination swept across the globe, Leahy still could not abandon his initial impressions of the Highlanders. He clung to a static image of them, the one he had formed years before. Insisting that they could not function without Australian rule, he lived out his life in New Guinea writing vituperative editorials against the country's demand for independence. He died a bitter, resentful man.

PICKRICKS AND PRINCIPLES

On July 3, 1964, three African-American men approached a restaurant in Atlanta, Georgia. The Pickrick was known for its fried chicken, but the three men wanted more than just a meal.

They had come as other blacks before them, to be served in a segregated restaurant. Always they had been turned away, their entrance barred by the owner, Lester Maddox, but thanks to a recent act of Congress, the pressure on Maddox to desegregate had just been substantially increased. A crowd of Maddox's supporters now gathered outside the Pickrick. Wielding ax handles, they formed a human barricade. At their head stood Maddox, a balding, middle-aged man with horn-rimmed glasses and a pistol at his side.

"I'll use ax handles, I'll use guns, I'll use my fists . . . I'll use anything," Maddox said. The Pickrick was Maddox's life, and he had no intention of allowing Negroes to enter his establishment. Laying down the law, Maddox swore to the black men, "If you live 100 years you'll never get a piece of fried chicken here."[1] Maddox's time frame, it turned out, was off by about a century. Maddox's story is about more than just pure racism. The case is also one of static cling.

On August 10, 1964, the Fifth Circuit Court of Appeals ruled that Maddox was in violation of the new Civil Rights Act. The court ordered that he desegregate the Pickrick at once. Maddox and his wife had refused to serve blacks for years. An avowed Christian, he was convinced that the Bible called for racial segregation. He maintained that the federal government was wrong to force him to run his business differently from how he saw fit. Maddox, like so many of his contemporaries, could not see that the times had irrevocably changed. Rather than admit blacks into the Pickrick, he shut down the restaurant and sold it six months later. The new owners, who were some of Maddox's former employees, reopened the business as the Gateway. They served both blacks and whites.

Stripped of the Pickrick, Maddox was left to seek a new career. The choice was obvious. In 1966, just two years after the nationally observed ax-handle affair, Maddox ran for governor. At that time, Georgia's election rules granted the state legislature the power to select the governor from the two top candidates. Maddox had finished second to a Republican, and since the legislature was dominated by Democrats, it selected him. Then, to the surprise and confusion of most, Governor Maddox appointed more African-Americans to government positions than any previous Georgia governor. He named the first African-American to the State Patrol and the first to the State Board of Corrections. Maddox also pushed for prison reform, a move popular with African-American voters. When faced with the overwhelming force of federal law against segregation, Maddox partly bowed to changing times.

Julian Bond, chairman of the NAACP from 1998 to 2008, remembers dealing with Governor Maddox in the sixties. Bond served several terms in the statehouse after being elected one of Georgia's first African-American representatives in 1965. He remembers the governor being quick to get things done, even on issues of civil rights.

But the old Lester Maddox never fully vanished. Leading Georgia's delegation at the 1968 Democratic Convention, he worked against the party's efforts to further civil rights. He also refused to fly state flags at half mast when Martin Luther King Jr. was killed.

In the 1960s Lester Maddox could not face the new South, and the new America, that was emerging all around him. He had invested so much of himself not just into the Pickrick, but into a set of values. When his society rejected those values, Maddox could not shift gears. He was ready to fight that change with axes, fists, and fury. If it had just been about racism, Maddox could never have appointed blacks to important positions when he was governor. What forced Maddox to close down the restaurant that meant so much to him was his inability to accept that times had changed for good.

Other southern politicians who had been ardent segregation-ists, such as U.S. senator Strom Thurmond, abandoned their old views when they saw that times had changed. Thurmond, who once delivered the longest filibuster in U.S. Senate history when he opposed the Civil Rights Act, later accepted that segregation was finished and employed blacks on his own staff.[2] Maddox, however, kept his Pickrick principles alive, long after that shop had shut its doors for good.

In 1990, hoping for one last hurrah, Lester Maddox reen-tered politics in an unlikely bid for governor. Maddox was challenging the front-runner, Zell Miller, who had served as his executive secretary when Maddox was governor back in the sixties. Maddox was trounced. Despite having enacted some progressive measures as governor, he was forever viewed as the ax-wielding Pickrick owner of his past. And for good rea-son. As late as 2001, two years before his death, he still clung to the essential tenets of his old beliefs. In an interview with the Associated Press, he admitted that he thought forced desegrega-tion was wrong and that he wanted his race preserved. He died still wedded to the principles of Pickrick.

The Weak-Kneed Giant

If ever there was a business in America that should have flour-ished in the computer era, IBM was it. For most of the twenti-eth century, International Business Machines held a virtual monopoly on the computer market. The mainframes its engi-neers constructed and the research its scientists performed had advanced America's economic, scientific, and military growth. IBM had even played a part in constructing the nation's social safety net. In the 1930s the federal government employed IBM to help develop the Social Security system, which would keep millions of elderly Americans out of poverty in their golden years. IBM took similar care of its own employees, several hundred thousand of them in 160 countries, granting them comfortable pension and benefit plans. With a market-dominant position and a powerhouse of knowledgeable workers, IBM should have dwarfed its closest competitors.

Yet by the early 1990s, IBM's fate was very much in doubt. Business watchers spoke of IBM as a dinosaur whose final extinction was only a matter of time. As smaller, more dynamic computer companies rose to prominence in the 1980s and '90s, IBM saw its market share shrink, its revenues plummet, and its future prospects darken. That was when Louis Gerstner arrived as the new CEO and staged a turnaround.[3]

Gerstner quickly discovered one of IBM's greatest weaknesses. After decades of success and market dominance, its employees had developed a self-destructive sense of static cling. The entire company had refused to adapt to the newly competitive computer industry. It simply had not acknowledged that conditions had dramatically changed. Management and labor no longer believed that competition was necessary. An inward-looking corporate culture had evolved. Divisions within the company battled with each other rather than battling actual competitors outside the company. Managers sought to protect their petty subdivision fiefdoms at the expense of the entire company's success. Too many of its managers saw threats only from within, not from without. One employee even sent Gerstner an e-mail within his first year at the helm explaining why combative language should be removed from Gerstner's speeches. The employee argued that fighting words are unhealthy and counterproductive to fostering a peaceful work environment. From upper management on down, IBM employees had been lulled into complacency, believing that IBM's dominant position simply existed as part of the natural order of things. Gerstner understood that businesses that remain static wither and die. In the fiercely competitive free market, only businesses with a fighting spirit survive.

To foster an outward-looking, competitive worldview, Gerstner instituted a bold series of changes designed to shatter the corporation's insularity. He began by delivering a hellfire, no-nonsense speech to the entire company, one that shocked and dismayed managers and employees alike. Gerstner flashed photos of the competition on a large screen above him. "Thousands of IBM employees have lost their jobs in the last few years," he shouted. "Who do you think did this to them? Was it an act of God?" No, Gerstner insisted. It happened because IBM had gone soft. It had forgotten how to fight for its market share. It had slept while its competitors gnawed away at its flesh and bones. All that, Gerstner declared, would now change.

True to his word, Gerstner institutionalized incentive structures that rewarded team players and punished petty turf mongers. The first thing to go was the "non-concurrence" policy. Believe it or not, IBM departments actually reserved the right not to comply with instructions from higher up the chain of command. If a department head did not like the decision made by higher-ups, he could just ignore it, thus rendering months or years of carefully researched plans defunct. Gerstner put an abrupt end to the absurdity of non-concurrence. He then revamped the employee benefits structure to bring it in line with their competitors. In short, Gerstner declared war on insularity and led IBM to an outward-looking worldview.

It was a risky approach. The IBM bureaucracy could have fought back, resisting his aggressive moves, but enough employees longed for success that the strategy had a chance to succeed.

Gerstner's gamble soon began netting huge returns. Within just a few years of his appointment as CEO, IBM's market share had begun to rise once again. Losses stopped; wasteful practices within the company were reduced or eliminated altogether. A team spirit was revived. The three key concepts he tried to instill throughout all levels of IBM—win, execute, and team— seeped into the company's collective mind-set and produced impressive results. By the end of Gerstner's tenure in 2003, IBM had staged one of the most successful turnarounds in American business history, thanks in large part to the adoption of a wiser worldview.

Gerstner's success with IBM can be measured in many ways: by percentage of market share, stockholder value, revenue streams, and more. But his greatest success came in prying his company free from static cling. By imbuing a corporate behemoth with the stark awareness that business conditions had fundamentally changed, Gerstner helped turn deterioration into vibrancy. Lou Gerstner recognized the static cling that was stifling IBM's competitiveness. Once he became aware of it, and made others aware as well, he was able to break free of that particular cognition trap and set the entire corporation back on track. Gerstner did not possess a nuanced expertise in computers. His knowledge of mainframes and the inner workings of IBM's other products was limited at best. What he did possess was the imagination to see that a fundamental shift had occurred in the computer industry. No longer could IBM operate as it had done for decades. If it wanted to survive and flourish, the company would have to adapt to a changing world.

IBM provides an uplifting lesson that even large, unwieldy organizations can change their worldviews. And if IBM can do it, surely other businesses can, too. For better or worse, shaking free from static cling usually has to start at the top. It takes a leader who is willing to challenge the fundamental views not just of those outside his organization, but of those within it as well.

BROADCASTING CHANGE

On May 7, 2007, Rupert Murdoch entered the Hudson Theater in New York City and faced the cameras. This was the first time he had ever addressed every employee of his global media empire. Hoping to reach every level of his corporation, Murdoch declared, "This is about changing the DNA of our business to reimagine how we look at energy."

One of the keys to business acumen is the ability to avoid static cling. Lou Gerstner overcame the cognition trap that had already hamstrung IBM, but Rupert Murdoch has repeatedly kept his company ahead of the curve. Years earlier he had proved this by launching the Fox News Channel to compete with the three major established networks. He proved it again by purchasing the Web site MySpace before it exploded in popularity. In 2007, he proved it once again by anticipating a dramatic shift in the popular opinion about the environment. That change, he believed, was more than just a passing trend. Murdoch had become convinced that global climate change needed to be addressed, and he directed his vast News Corporation to adapt.

The News Corp. CEO told his employees that the company's use of energy was inefficient and harmful to the environment. By printing and publishing newspapers, producing films, broadcasting television signals, and operating twenty-four-hour newsrooms, its emission of greenhouse gases was enormous. The company's carbon footprint in 2006 measured 641,150 tons—a stunning amount of energy to be consumed by a single corporation. Murdoch announced his intention to make all his businesses carbon-neutral by 2010. It was a bold initiative.

The plan involved transforming News Corp. to a green-friendly company. Energy-saving lightbulbs would replace the wasteful ones currently in use. Solar-powered golf carts would be used to transport workers around production lots. Hybrid vehicles would be used for longer business travels. Fox News would move into a new studio, the company's first U.S. building to be officially recognized as achieving excellence in environmental design. Some offices would now heat their water with solar panels. Others would draw their energy from hydroelectric plants, no longer from coal. Murdoch had become a true believer in the dangers of climate change, perhaps because his home country of Australia has been feeling its effects more powerfully than America. But Murdoch was not done yet.

"We can set an example," he insisted. "And we can reach our audiences. Our audience's carbon footprint is ten thousand times bigger than ours. That's the carbon footprint we want to conquer." Knowing that his Fox News company and his many other news providers around the world have a potent impact on people's attitudes and opinions, Murdoch determined to use his influence to promote sensible environmental management. "We cannot do it with gimmicks," he told his media executives. "We need to reach them in a sustained way. To weave this issue into our content—make it dramatic, make it vivid, even sometimes make it fun. We want to inspire people to change their behavior." Even if all these efforts caused his audiences to reduce just 1 percent of their energy consumption, he said, this would have a dramatic effect on the planet.

Murdoch's plan was driven not only by altruistic concerns for the environment, but also by sound business sense. Saving energy saves money. Recognizing that the earth's climate was changing and responding to that change made sense for the planet as well as for profits.

After outlining the steps that News Corp. would take and why it must take them, Murdoch then said something truly remarkable to his thousands of employees. Some of his own star broadcasters on his Fox News Channel, such as Sean Hannity, have consistently opposed the notion of global warming. Hannity has argued that because some scientists once believed that the earth was cooling, today's consensus that the planet is warming cannot be trusted. In other words, any previous incorrect scientific views invalidate any current conclusions. Murdoch, having weighed the evidence in a pragmatic, businesslike fashion, believes otherwise. He had to confront the fact that some of his own employees suffer from static cling. "Now there will always be journalists . . . including some of ours . . . who are skeptical, which is natural and healthy. But the debate is shifting from whether climate change is really happening to how to solve it." With those words, the farsighted CEO reframed the discussion. He cast the doubters of climate change as static clingers, while positioning the confronters of that change as problem solvers. It was a clever tack, followed by an initiative to reward employees financially for their ideas on other ways the company could reduce its energy use. Murdoch meant business, and his business now meant change.

SEEDS OF DOUBT

So far, we've seen some examples of how static cling can weaken businesses and ruin lives. We've also seen how overcoming it can help businesses to prosper and individuals to succeed. I want now to show you two unusual cases that break the mold. In both these stories, the people who were caught by static cling suffered personally, but their resistance to changing times actually had some positive effects for others. Don't misinterpret these stories to mean that static cling is a good thing. Instead, understand that there are occasions when resisting change is the right thing to do, even though the costs can be severe. History is fluid, and sometimes the people who seem out of touch are in fact far ahead of their times.

Percy Schmeiser and his wife owned some fourteen hundred acres on the windy Saskatchewan plains of Canada. Schmeiser had been farming that same land since 1947, when he took over from his father. By 1998 he and his wife were thinking about retirement, but then the world's largest agrochemical corporation filed suit against them. The odds of beating Monsanto in a lengthy trial were slim, and the costs to the elderly couple would be severe. The prudent course would have been to settle out of court, but Percy Schmeiser was not prudent. He had his own form of static cling. He could not accept that power had long ago passed from individual farmers to the hands of Goliath corporations.

The Schmeisers were known as seed savers. Each season they kept some of the best seeds from each harvest's canola crop and planted them the following year. (Canola is also known as grape seed.) Monsanto alleged that some of Schmeiser's canola crops contained the genes from Monsanto's Roundup Ready genetically modified seeds. The independent farmer claimed he had never purchased any genetically modified organism (GMO) seeds, never used any, and in fact never wanted any. Because the Schmeisers were seed savers they had been breeding the most resilient, best-tasting grape seeds for decades. They were opposed to GMOs and believed they were unnecessary. To them, the presence of Monsanto's seeds was a contamination of the crops that they had spent their lives developing. But to

Monsanto and the Canadian courts, the Schmeisers' lifetime of seed saving didn't matter. Roundup Ready was found on the Schmeisers' land, and the corporation now laid claim to all the couple's profits.

But if Schmeiser had not planted the GMO seeds himself, how could they have gotten on his land? Schmeiser found that a neighbor had been using Roundup Ready, and the winds had blown some of the seeds onto his own fields. The contamination could also have come from birds carrying any part of the neighbor's plants onto Schmeiser's crops, or bees could have pollinated plants from both crops, or even the rain could have caused the tiniest bits of the neighbor's GMO plants to infect his land. All it takes is for genetically modified DNA to reach a field, and the germination process can begin.

Monsanto had brought similar suits against scores of farmers before. Given the company's deep pockets and teams of high-paid lawyers, most farmers settled out of court, relinquishing their crops to the company or converting to GMO seeds, which must be purchased anew each year from Monsanto. Monsanto's contracts with farmers stipulate that seed saving is strictly forbidden and punishable by hefty fines or court battles. Making farmers buy new seeds annually ensures the company a steady revenue stream, a reasonable expectation given the company's costly investment in genetic research.

Schmeiser had not just saved seeds; he and his wife had saved for their retirement. They knew that fighting Monsanto in court would be long and draining. And it was. The suits continued for five years and their expenses totaled more than $300,000 in court costs and legal fees. All of the Schmeisers' $200,000 savings had to be spent.

In 2004 the Canadian Supreme Court ruled 5 to 4 that Schmeiser had infringed on Monsanto's patent. Monsanto was seeking more than $100,000 in damages, but because Schmeiser had not profited from the GMO crops the court dropped all penalties against him. The court ordered both sides to pay their own legal expenses. "This could have broken us financially," Schmeiser said. "At least we have a roof over our heads."[4]

Schmeiser's practice of seed saving, something that he and countless other farmers have done for centuries, now risks patent infringement. Because Monsanto forbids farmers from saving its GMO seeds, the company eliminates a key way in which farmers can save money from season to season. The cost of purchasing new seeds annually could be especially burdensome to farmers in the developing world. When its GMO seeds spread accidentally to natural crops, they also eradicate that crop's purity; in effect, free-market rules have enabled a corporation to privatize a piece of nature.

There is another threat both to farmers and the food supply itself. Monsanto has developed what are called terminator seeds, which produce plants that cannot reproduce. By spreading these seeds the company ensures that none of its customers can save seeds for future planting. No one knows what the effect might be if the terminator seeds pollinate untainted crops. Some in the scientific community fear that terminator seeds could spread beyond control. They worry that wind, rain, birds, or insects could transmit the genes and inadvertently terminate large portions of the natural food supply.[5] Monsanto insists that these fears are unwarranted. The company's own scientists are certain that nothing can possibly go wrong.

Percy's Schmeiser's static cling—his refusal to accept the fundamental change in modern agrobusiness—had the unexpected result of transforming him into an international icon for farmers' rights. His rejection of GMOs has earned him notoriety in Europe and Japan, where GMOs are banned for safety

reasons. In his seventies, Schmeiser has traveled to countries in Europe, Asia, and Africa, speaking to farmers about the dangers posed by agrochemical corporations, their tactics, and their products. Schmeiser's static cling cost him years of hardship and his life savings. But it has also inspired a global movement, raising awareness and challenging the way the farming business is done. Though the burdens on him and his wife have been high, the benefits to others may one day be even higher.

CURRENT COSTS

In the introduction I told the story of how Nikola Tesla and Thomas Edison battled over the future of electrical current. Edison, who suffered from static cling, was unable to accept that the modern world was outgrowing his system of direct current. He refused to adapt his products to the immense power of alternating current. There's an unfortunate postscript to that tale. For all his uncanny foresight, Tesla, too, it turned out, had his share of static cling.

Tesla was a dreamer. He was not committed foremost to profit; he wanted instead to power machines that would ease the burden of labor. In the depression of 1893 the Westinghouse Corporation looked like it might go under. The royalties that Westinghouse had to pay Tesla could have made him a billionaire. Paying him, however, might have bankrupted the company. Seeing no other option, George Westinghouse visited Tesla in his laboratory and explained the situation. Few people would have done what Tesla did. He produced his copy of the legally binding contract he had with Westinghouse, thanked his employer for his friendship in the past, and tore the contract to shreds. He did this on one condition: that Westinghouse would spread Tesla's designs throughout the world.

Tesla sacrificed a fortune, but he never believed this act would leave him penniless. Tesla clung to a patrician sense of the world. When gentlemen did business, they honored an unspoken code. With all the value his inventions could offer, Tesla assumed there would always be sponsors—even if an immediate profit could not be obtained. But the days when Tesla could expect unconditional patronage were passing. What Mark Twain had dubbed the Gilded Age was fading, too.

Without the royalties from his most lucrative invention, Tesla's financial health steadily declined. In later years the legendary inventor was reduced to begging his former sponsors for support just to cover the most basic needs. Most of them turned him away. Out of pity, not to mention concern for its public image, the Westinghouse Corporation decided to pay Tesla's rent to avoid the ignominy of having the famed inventor go homeless. Tesla died a poor man, unable to discern that the changing times would rob him of financial backing. In the end, he sacrificed his personal profit to ensure that millions of others would prosper from his creations. Static cling cost Tesla a personal fortune, but his willingness to do good still touches our daily lives. Edison was worth $12 million by the time he died, and his name is synonymous with electric light.[6] Tesla, in contrast, has been largely overlooked by the general public, but it is alternating current that powers the world.

Chapter 8

COGNITION-TRAPPED IN IRAQ

O N SEPTEMBER 20, 2001, President George W. Bush stood before a joint session of Congress to declare war on terror. The country's shock and grief from 9/11 were still fresh. Americans needed to know how they could move forward. The president could not have had a more receptive audience. In a striking show of unity, Senate Majority Leader Tom Daschle (D-SD) and Minority Leader Trent Lott (R-MS) each crossed the aisle to sit with their opposing political party. The president embraced House Minority Leader Richard Gephardt (D-MO). Britain's prime minister, Tony Blair, had flown in from London to be on hand. Dignitaries, cabinet members, and survivors of the 9/11 attacks were all present. The nation was watching. It was the most important speech of Bush's career. Every word counted. He needed to reassure and uplift an entire nation, and he did.

It was a stirring address. The president outlined the goals in a global struggle. Good would battle evil, and justice would be done. And then the president uttered one of the most memorable lines of the night. "Every nation, in every region, now has a decision to make. Either you are with us, or you are with the terrorists."

As a guiding principle it lacked nothing in boldness and clarity. There was of course a problem. Those words reflected a mind-set caught in a cognition trap. Dividing the world into two camps left no room in between. It reduced geostrategic complexities to the most simplistic calculus. It harkened back to the Cold War's fear-filled flatview.

Afghanistan's Taliban regime was clearly with the terrorists. They harbored al-Qaeda, provided sanctuary for their training camps, and refused to assist with the capture of Osama bin Laden. Iraq, however, did not fit neatly into the president's Manichean flatview. There is some evidence that Saddam Hussein's regime conducted limited discussions with Iran regarding joint anti-U.S. activities,[1] and there is further evidence that Iraq's actual involvement with global terrorist networks was either insignificant or nonexistent.[2] Saddam Hussein had had twelve years since his defeat in 1991 to ally with anti-American terrorist organizations, yet he appears not to have done so. The reasons might include his dislike of Islamist ideology, his preoccupation with firing on U.S. and allied pilots in the no-fly zone, and his fear of retaliation by the United States if he were linked to an attack on U.S. soil with weapons of mass destruction. Having seen how easily his forces were defeated in the first Gulf War, he may have been content not to provoke America's full wrath again, but instead to limit his opposition to the U.S. to talking tough and harassing American planes over Iraqi airspace.

By constructing a Cold War–like flatview, in which nations were placed in either a "with us" or an "against us" camp, both policy makers and parts of the American public came to perceive Iraq as more threatening to U.S. security than it actually was. This mind-set eased the way for another cognition trap over the issue of weapons of mass destruction (WMD).

When Douglas Feith, the assistant to Secretary of Defense Donald Rumsfeld whom I profiled in the introduction, said that expertise is not the same thing as sound judgment, he was absolutely right. Expertise in any given single area is not enough to guarantee either prudent policies or the avoidance of blunders. But why isn't it? If someone spends years or decades of his or her life studying the intricacies of a region, an issue, or a puzzle, why shouldn't that expert be better positioned to make good decisions?[3] One reason is that it's not *what* people know, or even what exactly they think, that ultimately matters in making judgment calls. Expertise is necessary—in fact, it is essential—but it is not sufficient. Far more important is *how* people approach and solve problems. It's how they think about the situations they face. And the way that people thought about America's actions in Iraq left the United States cognition trapped in the entire region.

Most blunders involve more than one cognition trap, but the tragic aspect of America's Iraq debacle is that *all* of the cognition traps outlined in this book combined to sabotage America's success. After constructing a flatview of the post-9/11 world, policy makers next fell victim to the most common cognition trap in war.

MIRROR IMAGING

When Secretary of State Colin Powell delivered his lengthy address on Iraq to the United Nations Security Council, he hoped to persuade America's allies that Iraq possessed WMD. "What's being hidden? Why?" Powell asked rhetorically. "There's only one answer to the why: to deceive, to hide, to keep from the inspectors."

One of the key mistakes that policy makers and politicians alike committed over Iraq's supposed WMD was to assume that Saddam Hussein would behave as Americans would. If Saddam had nothing to hide, many people assumed, then why would he not admit inspectors into Iraq to show the world his empty arsenal? That is, after all, what most Americans would expect one to do if falsely accused. But this view overlooked Saddam's perspective. The Iraqi dictator may well have had nothing to hide and therefore had to hide it. If he believed that part of his power rested on the image of a strongman with the ability to deploy WMD at will, then exposing himself to the world as impotent might, in his mind, have been tantamount to abdication.

Assuming that the senior officials in the Bush administration genuinely believed that Iraq possessed weapons of mass destruction and felt threatened by them, mirror imaging may have made understanding Saddam's behavior impossible. The Iraqi dictator would not, and probably could not, act as American leaders might have done if pressed to open their national security secrets to world inspection, but at this point, the American invasion was already long in planning.

CAUSEFUSION

When the ancient Romans assumed that bad swamp air caused malaria, they were not completely off base. It was not the air but the mosquitoes carrying the malaria virus that caused the disease. Since there were more mosquitoes around the swamps, you were more likely to contract malaria if you ventured too close to the swampy regions. It was an understandable case of causefusion. Perhaps in a similar way, since Iraq was America's most familiar enemy, it seemed reasonable to many people that Saddam Hussein must have been involved. Unfortunately, they were mistaken. Americans mistook the immediate cause of 9/11: al-Qaeda, with Taliban support. America's enemies were more numerous than they realized. With some encouragement from the

Bush administration, the public became easily causefused. In such a state, it was easier to win converts to cure-allism.

CURE-ALLISM

In his second inaugural address, President Bush declared, "It is the policy of the United States to seek and support the growth of democratic movements and institutions in every nation and culture, with the ultimate goal of ending tyranny in our world." With these words the president began to proselytize a cure-allism dogma. This time the panacea was not shock therapy or open capital markets. Democracy itself became the cure-all, and the Wilsonian ideal of spreading it throughout the world was America's new aim. Democracy, of course, is a noble aim. The problem is not the desire to help other countries become democratic. The problem is that cure-allism is a dangerous dogma. The ideal of transforming all nations into democracies embodies a flatview by seeing democracy as a binary function, as either on or off, democratic or unfree. Democracy is not an end point but a process, and all countries have degrees of democracy. They move along a continuum, becoming more or less free over time. And they do not move in only one direction. Americans have too often viewed their own country as the prototype of a healthy democracy. American statesmen have often thought that if they can re-create their own institutions in other countries— exporting free elections, multiple parties, a free press, and a system of checks and balances—then those other countries will be democracies just like the United States. But since democracies take generations to evolve, grafting on American-style institutions provides only the trappings of democracy, not its substance. In theory, and perhaps even in practice, Iraq could become a vibrant democracy. But believing that America has the power to make it resemble the American prototype requires conversion to cure-allism.

The converts to cure-allism in Iraq also tried to apply their theory that the market can remedy all ills. The Coalition Provisional Authority (CPA) was established to govern Iraq until elections could transfer power to Iraqis. During the CPA's rule, a number of American ambassador L. Paul Bremer's aides tried to push through American-style privatization plans. The biggest economic problem in post-Saddam Iraq was unemployment. Some estimates put the jobless rate at 40 percent. Surprisingly, the CPA's economic plan said almost nothing about unemployment. Instead they focused on privatizing Iraqi industries. In theory, selling off Iraq's industries to private investors would make them more efficient and ultimately create jobs. The CPA wanted to rush the privatization process through without Iraqi consent. But what if the new Iraqi government that would take power after elections did not want its industries sold off to foreign corporations? It would be too late to reverse the sales. The *Washington Post* journalist Rajiv Chandrasekaran describes in chilling detail the CPA's efforts to push through its privatization cure-alls.[4] He relates one episode in which a newly arrived economic aide, Tom Foley, tells a contractor that he intends to privatize *all* of Iraq's state-owned enterprises within thirty days. When the contractor informed him that this would violate international law, which prevents occupation governments from selling state assets, Foley allegedly replied, "I don't give a shit about international law. I made a commitment to the president that I'd privatize Iraq's businesses."

The privatization plans foundered, not for a lack of ardent advocates in the CPA, but because of the Iraqis' unwillingness to comply. Economics is not a science and never can be. Whenever humans are involved their differing historical and cultural backgrounds will affect any economic plan. That's what Jeffrey Sachs discovered when he applied his "shock therapy" theory to Russia, and it's what the IMF discovered when it deregulated capital markets and cut government subsidies in the Asian financial crisis. When the CPA experts tried to force their theories onto Iraq, the reality of Iraqi intransigence ground them to a halt. "They sort of looked at us like clowns that kind of came in there and had ideas and concepts that never had any assets to back it up," one CPA official told Chandrasekaran. "It's like one man walking into a country, a hugely militarized country, with a piece of paper and saying 'This piece of paper now says I run the country' and that country has 24 million people with weapons. They're just going to look at him and go, 'Oh, why don't you sit down over there in the corner, crazy guy.' That's what the Iraqis were like to us. They were like, 'There's three of you. There's 150,000 of us [in the Economics Ministry] . . . you haven't seen most of the factories. Why do you think that you're going to make any of the decisions? So they just kept doing their thing, and we sort of played in our little imaginary world over at the CPA."

INFOMANIA

Before cure-allism seized the CPA, another cognition trap was gripping the highest officials back in Washington. Whenever Secretary Rumsfeld briefed members of the White House on military plans, he made certain to retrieve the slides he had shown and return them to the Pentagon, ensuring that others could not retain copies for their future reference. Rumsfeld allegedly once instructed Frank Miller, the senior defense aide on the National Security Council staff, not even to take notes at these briefings. Miller had previously served in the Pentagon and had been trusted with some of America's most sensitive nuclear secrets. Apparently, Rumsfeld did not even want to empower high-level aides with records of the information he possessed. As the authors Bernard Trainor and Michael Gordon wrote, "The National Security Council was a system that assumed senior officials would cooperate and share information with their counterparts and which rarely cracked down when they did not . . . Rumsfeld fully understood the weakness of the NSC system and took advantage of it."

To combat the defense secretary's infomisering—one type of infomania—the then national security adviser, Condoleezza Rice, frequently sent her own spies to the Defense Department in hope of surreptitiously collecting the information she and her staff needed to do their jobs. Sometimes she shared her findings with Secretary of State Colin Powell. One of Frank Miller's aides, Marine colonel Tom Greenwood, told Trainor and Gordon: "I would put on my uniform and go to the Pentagon as though I was visiting friends. I'd then pick up the material we were looking for and spirit it back to the White House." Trainor and Gordon concluded that Rice and Powell were waging a type of guerrilla war "to counter Rumsfeld's fetish for control."[5]

This infomisering by the defense secretary is not at all uncommon in government. In the run-up to a major war, however, it limits the free flow of information necessary for formulating the wisest possible policies. Information sharing within a government headed for war is not a matter of polite etiquette, practiced between bureaucrats in order to play nice. In the case of war planning, if infomisering results in unsound strategies, it can needlessly cost lives. So, too, can the other type of infomania: infovoiding.

On January 9, 2003, scarcely more than two months before

the U.S. invasion of Iraq, retired army general Jay Garner was in Manhattan delivering a report to the private corporation for whom he was working at the time when his cell phone rang. The caller was Doug Feith, the undersecretary of defense. Feith asked Garner to assemble a team to oversee Iraq's reconstruction if a war should take place. Garner had been chosen to head the new office because of his experience resettling Kurds who had been displaced after the first Gulf War. The general accepted the job with remarkably little time to prepare.

By the third week of February, Garner had compiled his newly formed Office of Reconstruction and Humanitarian Affairs (ORHA) and launched his first major interagency review. Calling together several hundred officials from the relevant government departments, Garner led a two-day conference at the National Defense University in Washington to discuss all necessary postwar plans. The two-day event was so packed with representatives from Defense, State, Justice, the military's central command (CENTCOM), and other government agencies that meetings were standing-room-only. One of those in the room was Tom Warrick. Warrick spoke out repeatedly at this meeting, demonstrating a surprising degree of knowledge about what to expect once the military phase of invasion had ceased. Garner had never met Warrick before this moment. He was duly impressed, and for good reason. Tom Warrick was the State Department official in the Bureau of Near Eastern Affairs who headed the "Future of Iraq" study, which had been under way at the State Department since April of 2002, when an invasion appeared likely. Some two hundred exiled Iraqi lawyers, engineers, businesspeople, and other experts contributed to the $5 million study, which foresaw the likelihood of widespread looting and a breakdown in electricity, water, and other critical infrastructure, and correctly assessed the challenges to building a cohesive civil society. After the meeting concluded, Garner approached Warrick, introduced himself, and, after learning about the "Future of Iraq" project, asked Warrick to join his team. With Warrick and his extensive plans at their disposal, the postwar reconstruction of Iraq might avoid some obvious blunders, the general must have believed.

Shortly thereafter, Garner attended a meeting with Defense Secretary Rumsfeld, who asked Garner to remain behind once the others left. According to General Garner, Rumsfeld told him to fire Tom Warrick. Incredulous, Garner explained that Warrick possessed a tremendous cache of information on Iraq's postwar needs. Having him at ORHA, Garner assured the defense secretary, would help smooth the reconstruction process. Rumsfeld was unmoved. He told Garner that this decision emanated from levels of the government that he could not question.

The next morning, Garner informed Warrick of his exchange with Rumsfeld. Warrick packed up his office and left, taking with him the hard drive containing the extensive "Future of Iraq" study. ORHA was thus deprived of valuable information—data that could have aided America's postwar efforts and might even have saved Iraqi and American lives.

"I thought Tom Warrick was a very, very astute, very competent guy. But I was not able to get him on the team," Garner later told PBS's *Frontline*. When asked why he was not permitted to use Warrick or the State Department's studies, Garner replied simply: "I don't know. I don't know the answer to that. I was just told, and now it's just a decision they made that we're not going to bring Tom Warrick or his work on the team."[6]

The RAND Corporation, a private research institute established by the U.S. government as a source for independent policy analysis, studies every American military campaign in order to assess its successes and failures. After delving into the government's postwar planning for Iraq, RAND concluded that much of the postwar chaos that arose in Iraq was foreseen by the State Department, yet the Bush administration's inner circle did not want to confront this information, because it contradicted—and in fact undermined—the Defense Department's assumptions. RAND revealed an astonishing degree of infovoiding by both the Defense Department and the Office of the Vice President. Some of the blunders that have accompanied the postwar period in Iraq are a direct result of this intentional cutting off of alternative ideas. RAND's prescription for future postwar planning was simple: officials must institute "some process for exposing senior officials to possibilities other than those being assumed."[7]

EXPOSURE ANXIETY

All these cognition traps were already present in the prelude to invasion. Once America was in, the question was, under what conditions would it leave? One of the worst-case scenarios would have been to inspire a deep resentment among average Iraqis and inflame a violent insurgency.

Every war has its turning points, moments when a particular battle or event shifts the dynamics of the entire conflict. In Iraq that turning point was Fallujah. The scenes of the charred and mutilated bodies of four American contractors being danced on by Iraqi children demanded a response. The marines, who were in charge of Fallujah, had a plan. Major General James "Mad Dog" Mattis commanded the First Marine Division. Mad Dog's plan was anything but crazy. Rather than assaulting the entire city, Mattis and his staff laid out a series of steps to arrest or eliminate only the ringleaders behind the killings. It was a measured response with a good chance of success. Mattis was overruled.

Secretary of Defense Rumsfeld, Ambassador Bremer, and presumably President Bush as well all wanted a show of force. The gory scenes of mutilated Americans were a public relations coup for the insurgents and a humiliation for the Americans. The belief at the highest levels appears to have been that a failure to respond with overwhelming force would be seen as weakness. The civilian leaders, and even some of the top generals, took the counsel of Cleon and demanded a massive attack.

A strange and unfortunate lesson has been learned from Vietnam. Many people have come to believe that America lost that war because the civilian leadership prevented the military from employing overwhelming force. If the military had been allowed to escalate, they insist, the United States could have been victorious. America dropped three times the tonnage in bombs on Vietnam and Cambodia than it did on all of Europe during World War II. America used napalm, Agent Orange, and cluster bombs. More than three million Vietnamese died in the conflict, and the destruction of infrastructure was extraordinary. It is unclear how much more overwhelming American force could have been, short of a nuclear attack, which the American people were unwilling to tolerate. The main concern at the time was that any greater escalation would cause China to enter the war in full force. But even if American military force had been increased and China had not intervened, there is no evidence that this would have altered the war's outcome, and there is significant evidence that the North Vietnamese were willing to continue the fight no matter how much force the U.S. employed.

The doctrine of overwhelming force has become a case of cure-allism. Its advocates point to Germany and Japan during World War II as examples of its effectiveness. The cure-allism cognition trap occurs when people take a successful theory and apply it where it doesn't belong. Overwhelming force can be extremely effective in a conventional theater, good for annihilating the enemy's capabilities (its tanks, bases, and physical assets). But against an insurgency, overwhelming force can easily backfire by devastating civilians whose support is essential to success.

Fallujah was a cognition trap double whammy. The decision to use overwhelming force against the city was a type of cure-allism, but it was fueled by exposure anxiety. Parts of the American public, just like parts of the civilian and military leadership, feared for the national image. "I think we ought to kill every person who's responsible for the deaths of those Americans," TV commentator Tucker Carlson declared on *Crossfire*. "This is a sign of weakness. This is how we got 9/11. It's because we allowed things like that to go unresponded to."[8] These kinds of statements reflected, and probably furthered, exposure anxiety. When the specious cure-all of overwhelming force meets the insecure machismo of exposure anxiety, blunders are born and bred.

The battle for Fallujah was really two battles. The first began in April immediately after the Blackwater contractors were murdered, but it was aborted as soon as the costs to America's image became clear. The second occurred in November when the city had become ungovernable either by American or Iraqi National Guard forces. During the protracted campaign many insurgent leaders fled the city to neighboring towns and villages. This had the effect of expanding rather than isolating the insurgency. One soldier who fought in Fallujah told me, "We thought that Fallujah was the hornet's nest of the insurgency and that if we crushed it there we could destroy it for good. We were wrong."

An international aid worker I interviewed worked with Fallujah's internally displaced residents. While many in the field of humanitarian relief expected that Fallujans would flee Iraq to find safety in Jordan and surrounding countries, those cases were few. Most Fallujans, he told me, were housed and fed by the open arms of fellow Iraqis in Anbar province and Baghdad. "Fallujah brought Iraqis together in the way that 9/11 brought Americans together. It created a sense of solidarity and became a symbol of resistance. Everyone was supporting the Fallujah people because they saw them as the brave ones, the defiant ones standing up to the Americans. Fallujans did not want to turn in the foreign fighters because they thought that anyone who would kill an American is a good person. What was not anticipated was the effects of the attacks on civilians who suffered the most."[9]

After an intense and overwhelming bombardment, the marines gained control of the city. The battle was won. The insurgency, however, was just beginning.[10]

Static Cling

Once the conventional war was over and the United States had clearly won, American military strategy failed to adapt to the conflict's changing nature. Even as insurgent attacks on civilians and U.S. troops continued, the American military's response centered overwhelmingly on force protection. This was a perfectly understandable reaction. Naturally, commanders will retaliate if fired upon, and they should. The problem is that the military did not concentrate enough on securing the Iraqi population. As the extensive RAND Corporation study concluded, "In Iraq, senior military commanders focused too long on roadside bombs and their impact on U.S. forces, rather than on the safety of the civilian population."[11] This worked to the insurgents' advantage. Their strategy, and the strategy of most insurgencies, is to gain the support of the local population, either by propaganda, if possible, or by intimidation if necessary. Because the insurgents were able to target civilians in brutal fashion, local Iraqis were much slower to trust or assist coalition troops.*

Regardless of whether Iraq ultimately becomes a safe haven for terrorists, a failed state, or a stable, prosperous, and flourishing democratic nation, the first five years of America's occupation involved a dizzying cascade of cognition traps. If even just one of them could have been avoided, the entire misadventure might not have been as grim.

*For more on the U.S. Army's slowness to adapt to the changing environment in Iraq, see its own 720-page report produced by the Combat Studies Institute, part of the U.S. Army Combined Arms Center at Fort Leavenworth, Kansas.

Chapter 9

WORKING TOWARD WISDOM

SILVER CITY, NEW Mexico, was a quiet mining town in the 1950s, a safe place to raise a family. One very ordinary morning in 1957, Mrs. May sent her two children, Michael and Diane, ages three and four, to play in the backyard. Mike decided to make mud pies, so he rummaged in the old garage for containers. Soon he found the perfect object: a glass jar filled only with some caked powder. Unaware that the jar contained volatile chemicals, Michael decided to clean it out by submerging it in the nearby stream.

When the jar exploded in his hands, the force of the blast sent shattered glass ripping into his flesh. The local emergency room doctors were certain the boy would die from blood loss and critical lacerations. He was airlifted by helicopter to El Paso, Texas, where surgeons worked for hours to repair the tears and burns. At last the doctors reported that, miraculously, the boy would live, but he would remain forever blind.

Mike May grew up to live a full and varied life, founding business ventures, traveling around the world, becoming an award-winning downhill skier, and even working for a time for the CIA. Then one morning in 1999, he accompanied his wife to her optometrist appointment in San Francisco. The optometrist unexpectedly asked if he could also examine May's one remaining eye. (May's other eye had been removed after the accident and he wears a remarkably lifelike prosthesis in its place.) May agreed to be examined, and then the optometrist called in his colleague, an ophthalmologist. May was surprised by all the attention, since he knew there was nothing that could be done to change his condition. The doctors disagreed. Thanks to recent advances in stem cell treatments, it now seemed possible to restore May's vision after forty-three years of blindness. It would require two separate operations of stem cell and cornea transplants, but there was a 50 percent chance of success.

After several months of weighing the risks, May decided to go ahead with the procedure. Following a period of recovery, it appeared that the process had worked. May's visual acuity improved from total blindness to a measure of 20/100. His eye was nearly perfect. Michael May had become one of fewer than twenty people in history to have been born blind or been blinded early in life and then regain sight. He was interviewed on television shows and contacted by medical professionals wanting to learn more about his case. From a medical standpoint, it was a truly remarkable event. Unfortunately, May quickly discovered an unforeseen result.

Although May's restored eye was physically fine, he could not recognize faces. He had no trouble seeing motion or colors, but he could not distinguish men from women based on their faces. He could not interpret facial expressions, and he had almost no depth perception. A cube, for example, looked to him exactly the same as a square, unless the cube was placed in motion. May could recognize objects in their proper context, like the small, flat, rectangular device next to the television he understood as the remote control. But if the remote was sitting on the kitchen table, May was baffled by it. The problems May experienced were clearly not with his eye but with his brain. They were entirely problems of cognition.

After hearing about his case on TV, Dr. Ione Fine, a cognitive psychologist at the University of California, San Diego, called May and invited him to visit her laboratory. Fine, an expert in the neuroscience of visual perception, ran batteries of tests on May and puzzled over the case for months. Fine came to believe that the problem lay in May's brain plasticity. She and many other scientists believed that children develop uses for their billions of neural networks in their early years of growth. These networks are essentially assigned different tasks by the brain: some perceive color, others depth, and so on. Fine suspected that the neural networks May needed to perceive depth, recognize faces, and interpret other visual clues had been reassigned to perform other tasks after he lost his sight. Perhaps his brain had formed new networks to aid him in echo location, Braille reading, or other nonvisual duties. Fine decided to test her hunch with the aid of functional magnetic resonance imaging (fMRI).

The scientists slid May inside a body-length machine where magnetic pulses tracked his neural activity. Fine and her colleagues then flashed pictures of faces and other objects on a screen that May could view, and they registered which parts of his brain lit up during the test. Sure enough, when looking at pictures of faces, May's brain showed no activity in the proper regions. With a heavy heart, Fine related the disappointing news. May would never see like a fully sighted person. The science was irrefutable. The fMRI had spoken.

At first, May took the news pretty hard. He had lived an exceedingly rich, full life without vision, but now that he had experienced sight, it seemed an unfortunate loss. Back home in the Bay Area, he called Fine to double-check that he had understood her prognosis correctly. Would he really never be able to see like a normally sighted person? She regrettably confirmed her conclusions. Mike May's brain, not his eye, was the problem.

As May processed the news over several days, he began to think more deeply about how he thinks. His brain might be the problem, but maybe it could be part of the solution as well. What if there was another way to see? What if he could get around the problem of identifying people and things by other means? It occurred to May that his ability to categorize might hold the key.

May concocted an unorthodox and potentially fruitless plan, though it had behind it a highly imaginative idea. He began constructing hundreds of new categories for everyday objects, discarding some of his old ways of categorizing things and creating new ones. Batteries, he noticed, have a distinctive color combination: dark along their length, then a rusty copper color toward the top. Other batteries had slightly different colors, but they could be placed in the category of small, cylindrical metallic objects, smooth on one end and knobby on the other. May invented new types of categories for hundreds of items in the supermarket, from peanut butter to raisin bran, deciding what makes them distinctive and how they fit into his own particular scheme. And that is how it began. It was a laborious, cognitively taxing method, but with the help of his wife, Jennifer, May found that it worked—not always, and not perfectly, but enough to increase his ability to function with vision.

Next, he tried the same approach with people. How can you recognize a flight attendant? For most people, it's the uniforms as well as the faces that help us to find them on board. To May, these people on airplanes looked like all the other passengers. May asked the person sitting next to him to point out a flight attendant and describe what it was about her uniform that made her different from others on the plane. Later, before the flight began its descent, May spotted a woman with the characteristic clothing he had memorized and asked her when they were due to land. He had identified her correctly. The method was working.

Emboldened by his successes, May next devised an additional strategy. He realized that he had been assuming that his vision was all he could use in order to see. This seemed a reasonable enough assumption, but it didn't really make sense, especially in May's case. May, after all, had nearly perfect optics, yet he still could not see like a normal person. It was his brain, specifically his ability to process the information he was receiving through the eyes, that was impaired. May now realized that he could rely instead on his other senses, particularly his sense of touch, which had always helped him while he was blind. May had long since developed his senses of touch, hearing, and smell, simply by using them more than a sighted person would. Those other senses were not magically enhanced because of his blindness. They were just more attuned as a result of greater use. So May set out to incorporate his other, well-developed senses into the stream of visual data.

Entering a new room for the first time, May explored the area by touching the chairs and tables, walking around the area, and listening for audible clues to get a sense of his environment, just as he had always done while blind. At the same time, he allowed the visual information to come pouring in through his eyes. It was a remarkably holistic and sensible approach, though it might have looked a little odd to anyone watching this seemingly sighted man feel his way through a room. The effect, however, was immediate and positive.

May phoned Dr. Fine in San Diego to tell her about his success. She was duly impressed and very happy for him. May's case had brought her no small amount of celebrity and recognition within her field, and the two had developed a friendship. The science suggested that May would never see like a normal person, and this was correct. But May had the gumption to challenge the conclusion that he could not improve his condition through unconventional means. Mike May improvised a set of solutions to his problems, and while he has not become a fully functioning sighted person, he has increased his ability to use vision. Although his case is remarkably rare, the lessons of Mike May's success are relevant to us all.[1]

Many, if not all, of the blunders described in this book came about partly from reductive thinking. They happened when people oversimplified complex situations into mental sound bites. Sometimes they relied on simplistic models of countries, cultures, or genders. Sometimes they reduced complex causes to single events. And sometimes they avoided thinking about how others would react to their solutions altogether. Because reductionism is so dangerous, it would be foolish to offer any simplistic solutions for always avoiding blunders. There are no step-by-step instructions we can follow to guarantee success, but there are some general guidelines that can help.

Like Mike May, who challenged the mainstream thinking about his condition, the people in this book who avoided blunders tended to challenge the prevailing view. When Diodotus stood against Cleon, he was taking a real risk. Opinion was inflamed, vengeance was in the air, and Cleon had roused the Athenians' passions against their enemies. But Diodotus was not intimidated. He thoughtfully questioned Cleon's assertions, identified the inherent assumptions in his logic, and exposed the flaws in his thinking. In a similar way, President Eisenhower stood up to his entire cabinet over intervening in Dien Bien Phu. The president was not obstinate about his views; he was mindful. He listened repeatedly to his advisers' arguments, and he pointed out the weaknesses in their thinking. There was nothing messianic or idealistic in his reasoning.

There was only sober logic based on sound experience and substantial empathy for the perspective of colonized peoples. It was not about sympathy—Eisenhower did not necessarily fret about the plight of Vietnamese villagers. It was empathy, the ability to imagine how others might think. As Eisenhower realized, understanding how others think is not a good-natured act of kindly political correctness; it is essential to America's national security. Diodotus, Eisenhower, and others in this book who exhibited empathy and imagination also had the fortitude to challenge the dominant view.

Blunders are also more likely to occur, and we exacerbate them when they do occur, if we insist on absolute certainty. Just think about the cognition traps and the people who fell into them. The believers in cure-allism were convinced that their theories would work in all cases, even when they knew little about the people whom their theories would affect. The infomaniacs had no doubts that hoarding or shunning information would serve them best, even when a freer flow of information would have been easy to create. And on down the list, those who blundered usually felt wedded to unshakable beliefs. They feared uncertainty and clung dogmatically to their rigid views.

Mental flexibility, on the other hand, dramatically helped people accomplish their missions and achieve their goals. Mike May was willing to adapt his thinking about vision by learning to integrate the process of seeing with his other senses. By feeling some objects at the same time he looks at them, he can recognize things more clearly for what they really are. David Karp and Elizabeth Gilbert, two people who suffered terribly from depression, began by believing that their illness had a purely biological cause that therefore required a biological cure. As they opened themselves to alternative possibilities, they both found that multiple, nonchemical means could bring them great healing. King Mongkut of Siam showed tremendous flexibility. While other Southeast Asian leaders shunned an in-depth knowledge of the Europeans, convinced that their own societies' methods were sufficient for success, Mongkut accepted that the Europeans possessed potentially useful customs, technologies, and ideas. The Siamese king opened his mind to new ways of thinking, and this mental agility helped safeguard his country's freedom. Business leaders like Rupert Murdoch discovered that they would prosper by a willingness to change their views and practices. Murdoch's dramatic efforts to make his News Corporation energy-efficient for both fiscal and environmental reasons only occurred after he allowed himself the flexibility to consider that his earlier thinking was unwise. Similarly, as Ronald Reagan learned more about Soviet perceptions of nuclear war, he altered his earlier thinking about the USSR and was willing to adapt his policies. We sometimes call people who change their minds "flip-floppers," because we view changing one's mind as a sign of weakness or lack of conviction. People who constantly change their minds are of course unstable and not to be followed. But those who permit themselves to learn, who understand that their thinking can evolve as new information becomes available, are the ones more likely to succeed.

All these traits—mental flexibility, the willingness to question the majority view, the rejection of reductionism, and the development of empathy and imagination—require hard work. They don't come easily to anyone. They not only don't come easily, they also don't come naturally with age. These traits are the building blocks of wisdom, and they take conscious effort to assemble.

I think that Mike May's flexibility of mind is inspirational, so much so that I asked him to speak with me about his experience. I felt drawn to his story for several reasons. First, I could relate to some of his experiences because I am also blind. But more crucially, I admired his uncommon openness to changing the way he thinks, and I respected his willingness to do the long, hard work to bring that change about. This type of consciously cultivated open-mindedness is precisely what's needed to escape cognition traps.

"I really liked the scientists who studied me," May told me one afternoon in 2007. "I knew they'd done the science. But I simply had to believe there was another way." May thinks that much of life is about trade-offs and compromises. You figure out what you have to work with and what you don't. The process of relearning how to integrate his other senses with his new vision has come not over weeks or months, but years. The scientists themselves took about a year before they concluded that May would never get any better. Then it took May several more years before he came up with a "work-around." "It took a lot of trial and error before I had that 'Aha!' moment when I knew for certain I was on to something." He told me it was like learning a new language, constantly throughout the day, every day: mentally exhausting, yielding slow but discernible progress. "I'm not fluent with vision, but I'm now proficient at what I do with it."

May is still learning how to integrate his blindness skills into his cognition and visual perception. It has been a long, arduous effort, and he is still far from living like a sighted person. Being flexible enough to include his other senses has eased the way. He still uses a cane and guide dog to ensure he travels safely. He still cannot recognize faces, but his ability to read print has improved. If he traces the letters on a page with his fingers, a rough approximation of what he used to do when reading Braille, he can sometimes grasp the words. "This morning," he says, "I pulled out a box of cereal. I'm looking at the letters, expecting it to say raisin bran. I'm tracing the letters with my index finger and slowly, very slowly, it's coming. R . . . a . . . i . . . but then I just said the heck with it and just smelled it."

We have always been told that wisdom comes with age. The more experiences we accumulate, they tell us, the wiser we should be. I'm not so sure it really works this way. Wisdom may not actually be a product of experience alone. Some people might be born with a predisposition to better judgment, but the rest of us, I believe, have to grow wiser by hard work. The kind of work I mean is mental work: taking the time and trouble to watch out for rigid thinking. What the historical and contemporary stories in this book reveal is that individuals, businesses, and nations can improve their judgment by a conscious effort of retraining how they think. Like Mike May, we can question our own use of categories as we approach new problems. We can push ourselves to imagine more creatively how others might think differently from us. We can eschew reductive solutions and monocausal explanations. And we can watch out for our own prototypes and other people's, too. All these things are hard. It takes effort to step back from our situations and think about how we think. We all want easy answers, which is what cognition traps provide. But if we do nothing more than just keep cognizant of cognition traps, we can take a giant leap toward getting the things that matter most.

THE SQUARE WHO DREAMED

Two years after the chemical explosion that blinded Mike May, Rita Dwyer was also injured in a chemical accident. Unlike

May, Dwyer was not blinded. Instead she was nearly burned alive. She would have died for certain if a colleague had not had an inexplicable, recurrent dream.

On April 23, 1959, Dwyer was working for the reaction motors division of Thiokol Chemical Corporation, America's premier liquid rocket fuel manufacturer, whose Bell X-1 engine had been the first to break the speed of sound. She had worked for Thiokol during her undergraduate summers and then full-time for four years. One of the few women chemists in the aerospace field, at age twenty-five she was already coauthor of several patents on liquid and solid rocket propellants.

"I was doing pioneering research on a new compound," Dwyer told me, "and had no problems with it the day before. It looked like it had terrific potential as a fuel source." During a coffee break that April afternoon, Dwyer continued her experiments while most of her colleagues had gone to the cafeteria. "I was always extremely careful. I wore all my protective gear and followed safety procedures to the letter." But the materials Dwyer worked with were highly unstable. It was never determined exactly what caused the explosion. At one point in the experiment, Dwyer raised a glass shield to check on the components, and the entire concoction erupted. She was instantly engulfed in flames.

Dwyer's whole body was burning. Smoke and fumes filled the lab. As her protective gear melted, she ran but could not see through the dense clouds of blazing fuel. She tried pulling her lab coat over her head to smother the flames, but because her hands and arms were on fire, she only worsened the burns to her body. Her clothes were saturated with chemicals and broken glass. She tried dropping and rolling, but the floor itself was also burning. Panic-stricken, and on the brink of unconsciousness, she screamed for help, but her lab was empty. "I felt myself being sucked up into the air. That's the best I can explain it. I suppose it was one of those near-death experiences people talk about. I found myself thinking, 'Here I come, God, ready or not.'" Then she heard a voice and blacked out.

The voice belonged to Ed Butler, a fellow chemist who worked several labs down the hall. Butler knew exactly where Dwyer would be and what he had to do. Butler had been suffering from a recurrent nightmare for days prior to the event. Each night in his dream he heard an explosion down the hall and saw himself running to the lab and hesitating at the door in sheer terror. Then, each night, he would see himself finding Rita Dwyer, dragging her to safety, and extinguishing the flames. A trained scientist and a burly man of Irish descent, Butler had worked on the dockyards during his high school summers. He was a practical-minded, logical-thinking researcher. He had no interest in dreams and no patience for spacey ideas.

On the day of the accident, Butler was doing paperwork in his lab and had removed all his safety gear. With shirtsleeves rolled up, he would be completely exposed to the chemicals and flames. But when the explosion came, he knew immediately to run toward Dwyer's lab. He hesitated at the doorway and called out her name. Groping his way through the haze of smoke, Butler grabbed the only part of Dwyer's body not on fire, her foot, and dragged her to a deluge shower in the neighboring lab. Butler was the only person in the building close enough to help. If he hadn't responded, Rita Dwyer would have died.

Dwyer awoke in the arms of a technician, whom she assumed had saved her life. When she later wrote to thank him, the technician explained that it was Butler who had rescued her. Only months later did Butler tell Dwyer about the dreams. He had no explanation for them and felt embarrassed to discuss it.

Dwyer remained in the hospital for almost six months. She endured repeated skin grafts and reconstructive surgeries, but there was little the doctors could do. All mirrors were removed from the room. For months she had no idea what she looked like, but she assumed it had to be grim. When the doctors finally permitted visitors, one of her colleagues and his wife came to see her. Dwyer remembers sitting in a chair facing the door. When it opened and the couple looked in, the wife fainted on the spot. Later, one of Dwyer's friends came to the hospital hoping to lift her spirits. The friend took one look at Dwyer, turned, and bolted for the bathroom to throw up.

The years of recovery were painful in every respect. She needed repeated surgeries just to restore her basic functions. Returning to work was ultimately impossible. Socially she withdrew, unable to bear being seen in public. It took years for the emotional scars, if not the physical ones, to subside. Remarkably, Dwyer eventually regained her confidence, married, and raised three children. Soon after the accident, however, Dwyer confronted a very different problem, and it's here where her story becomes even more interesting for its lessons about cognition.

Dwyer wanted to understand how Ed Butler's dreams could have possibly been connected to her accident. It was a tough problem to solve, and like most challenging, complex questions, the situation was ripe for cognition traps. Dwyer could have easily fallen prey to causefusion, assuming a link between the man's dreams and her accident that was not warranted by the facts. She could have engaged in infovoiding, refusing to learn anything about dreams and assuming that it was mere coincidence. Coincidence, however, seemed unlikely. These were two singular events that coincided: Dwyer burning in a lab explosion and Butler's recurrent dream about it. To be sure, explosions are not unheard of in chemical labs dealing with volatile rocket fuels. But there were many scientists in the company, it was the only accident Dwyer had been in, and Butler specifically saw her repeatedly in his nightmare. Dwyer needed to know what it meant. Most scientists in her position probably would have adopted a flatview of the whole matter, reducing the world into rationalists and quacks, placing herself into the first category and relegating Butler to the other. But Dwyer was open to questioning her fundamental assumptions. Like the square in Edwin Abbott's *Flatland*, Dwyer allowed herself to withhold judgment until she had explored the matter more deeply.

Dwyer started reading everything she could about dreams. Unfortunately, there wasn't that much out there, from a scholarly standpoint, in the 1960s. She attended a few workshops in the seventies and continued to consume the available literature. In 1983, she had the idea of starting a dream study group for the Washington, DC, area, where she lives. There were no fees, just fellowship, a place people could come to talk about their dreams and share information. Then the following year she heard about a new organization being founded in San Francisco. The International Association for the Study of Dreams (IASD) dedicated itself to exploring the causes and significance of dreams. "Initially, I had no intention of going to their conference in California. I just joined the membership, because I was curious and wanted to learn more." But Dwyer did attend, and she has attended every conference since then. At age seventy-three, she is considered a founding angel of the organization.

In the association, Dwyer found an ever-growing number of men and women dedicated to understanding dreams. Their ranks include psychologists and psychiatrists, sleep researchers, anthropologists, teachers, ministers, artists and writers, healers, and many more. "We try to respect all these views," she says. "It's a lot of work, but it has definitely paid off." Opinion within the association on the causes of dreams is still as varied as the members themselves. Some insist that dreams are little more than the result of biochemical processes in the brain that occur naturally during sleep. They view the chemical changes as the cause and the images and sensations as their effects. Others hold that dreams are a subconscious attempt to resolve the problems from our conscious hours. And still others are convinced that dreams can be portals through time, allowing us to gain glimpses of the future and the past, from our own lives and the lives of others.

Obviously, no one yet knows exactly why dreams occur or what their contents really mean. And this is the crucial point of Dwyer's exploration. Dwyer and those who study dreams are avoiding blunders by embracing uncertainty—the most essential way to escape cognition traps. Embracing some uncertainty is necessary when the facts are not fully known or understood. "As a trained scientist," Dwyer says, "I was naturally skeptical of studying dreams. But later I came to see that we all adopt the paradigms of the day, and if science has no explanation for something, we just dismiss it. Now I realize that there's much more out there that we don't yet understand."

We could not abandon certainty in our lives even if we wanted to, and we should not try. All I am suggesting is that we make a realistic effort to slow our rush to judgment before all the relevant facts are in. If we could grow more comfortable with the uncertainty around us, our daily blunders would not be as great. All kinds of daily interactions would be altered if we suspended our insufficiently informed conclusions over why others act the way they do. Maybe women would be less quick to assume that men reading the newspaper at breakfast necessarily want to shut them out. Men would be slower to interpret women's comments on their appearance as criticism rather than concern. Doctors would be more circumspect when prescribing medicines before the cause of someone's illness is clear. Policy makers would be less certain that defeated peoples will throw flowers at their feet. And voters would be less ready to accept what politicians proclaim as truth.

Embracing uncertainty does not mean that we stop searching for solutions. It only means that we remind ourselves and each other that our explanations are often based on insufficient understanding. Keeping cognizant of our own uncertainty empowers us to qualify our claims and moderate the solutions we adopt. Even more, it forces us to keep an open mind when we confront complex conditions. Open-mindedness sounds simple enough, but if we have discovered anything in this book, it is how hard being open-minded really is. Earlier I suggested that the surest sign of a limited intellect is a closed mind. Having a limited intellect does not necessarily mean that such people are stupid. It just means that they are unable to stretch toward their full potential. It's a needlessly tragic way to live, especially when the condition is self-imposed.

After almost fifty years of investigation, Rita Dwyer still cannot explain Ed Butler's dream, though she knows it saved her life. What happened that day in 1959 remains a mystery, yet Dwyer stays committed to the search. "We should be trying to investigate with whatever methods work," she insists, "even if they don't conform to current scientific views." Dwyer may seem like an open-minded dreamer. Fortunately, she is not alone. You and I can also escape from Flatland. Just imagine the complexity beyond.

ACKNOWLEDGMENTS

So many hands helped shape this book. My agent, Will Lippin-cott, worked with me as a true partner in the effort, guiding it from the proposal stage through to publication. Few authors could have such a dedicated advocate as Will. My editor at Bloomsbury, Kathy Belden, kept me focused on writing for a general audience, and I thank her for it. To maintain balance, my academic colleagues at Berkeley and other institutes offered written feedback and talked me through many complex issues bearing on their expertise. Margaret Anderson and John Connelly served as sounding boards for some of the ideas I developed in these pages. Peter Zinoman and Hanh Tran provided invaluable assistance on Vietnam's history and politics. Archie Brown, Stephen Schuker and Marc Trachtenberg, and Matthew McKay all generously gave of their knowledge on Russia, the Cold War, and psychology, respectively. Douglas Porch, the faculty, and staff at the Naval Postgraduate School have been tremendously supportive of my work. Lieutenant General Robert L. Ord graciously shared his insights with me on leadership, soldiering, and combat. The Institute of International Studies contributed support toward this project, while Beverly Crawford, Gia White-Forbes, Junko Kiross, and the staff at Berkeley's Institute of European Studies have consistently made going to the office something I look forward to. Because of them, the institute has been a remarkably productive place from which to write. To our great sadness, Gerald Feldman, who first invited me to IES while he directed the institute, died of cancer before this book could be published. Gerry's dedication to truth in scholarship inspired us all. His high spirits and hilarious wit always made us eager for his presence. He is deeply missed.

I have been especially lucky to have friends in the Bay Area writing community, all of whom helped in many ways. Daniel Mason kindly read some early, unpolished chapters and offered excellent suggestions for refining both the style and the substance. Over Cheeseboard pizza and wine (and sometimes over more wine than pizza), Daniel, along with Sara Houghteling, Frances Hwang, and Rebecca Black, helped brainstorm cases of cognition traps. Jason Roberts and his colleagues at the San Francisco Writers Grotto invited me to present this project at one of their lunchtime discussions. They all exhibited the kind of sound advice that comes only from experience. Steve Levine and I have traded chapters as we both sought to strengthen our craft. I am grateful for his constructive comments and useful tips. One night at a dinner party, Marcie Vu sank her teeth into this project and would not let go. Even as we were leaving her place at two in the morning, she was still calling my cell phone saying, "How about this case?" That kind of enthusiasm always amazed me when, at parties or dinners, people suddenly whetted their appetites on cognition traps, serving up a buffet of blunders. I wish I could acknowledge them all.

Several research assistants made a significant impact on this work. Adam Radin and Aaron May at the Naval Postgraduate School were terrific at ferreting out factoids and sniffing out stories. Megan Adams proved that she will make an excellent historian herself when her graduate studies are complete. As with my previous book, my faithful reader, Stephanie Lo, read every word of the manuscript, applying her serious intellect to the task. Trudy Kuehner has proofread each of my books, and I am convinced she has a bionic eye. I am thankful to them all.

My friends are my treasures, and in writing this book I was reminded how rich I truly am. Once again, Dominic Hughes turned his mathematical mind to my writing. His remarkable gift for rigorous thinking often forced me to reexamine my choice of words. Julien Basch read through the original proposal and helped set me on a surer course. Kristin Rebien was so thorough in her reading that she caught even the subtlest of errors. Kristin, how do you manage to improve my choice of words when English is not your native tongue? *Du bist ein Genie.* Nil Demirçubuk, another nonnative phenom, frequently rendered my passages far more lucid and precise. Nil's mom, Şerpıl, nourished me many times with home-cooked Turkish treats. Thanks, Annem, for all the börek and baklava. Kamal Kapadia spent many hours with me over cakes and chai, talking me through cognition traps and their impact on international development. Speaking of food for thought, my many dinners with Bryan Bashin invariably turned to blunders—the topic, not the meals. These conversations generated ideas that found their way inside this book. Two friends deserve special mention, plus a prize for patience. While simultaneously founding the software company Loomia, Francis Kelly found the time to read nearly every chapter of my first full draft, offering copious, detailed, and exceedingly perceptive comments. Ben Price believed in this project from the start. He plowed through each version of the proposal and many of the subsequent chapters. His insights were always scrupulously reasoned and right on the mark. This book is much the better for their help. My family, of course, is my greatest support.

NOTES

Introduction: Keeping Current

1. For more on Nikola Tesla see Margaret Cheney, *Tesla: Man Out of Time* (New York: Prentice Hall, 1981), and Jill Jonnes, *Empires of Light: Edison, Tesla, Westinghouse, and the Race to Electrify the World* (New York: Random House, 2003). For more on Edison see Randall Stross, *The Wizard of Menlo Park: How Thomas Alva Edison Invented the Modern World* (New York: Crown, 2007).

2. Although the Italian inventor Marchese Marconi initially received credit for inventing the radio, the U.S. Supreme Court ultimately settled the matter in Tesla's favor.

3. In *Tesla: Man Out of Time*, Margaret Cheney asserts that Edison admitted his mistake before he died. I find no persuasive evidence of this. As late as 1907, Edison still maintained that AC presented dangers to the public. See "Edison Condemns High Voltages," *Newark Advertiser*, December 30, 1907. Paul Israel, director of the collected Edison papers held at Rutgers University, told me in a telephone interview in March 2007 that he believes that Edison never fully accepted that AC was the better current.

4. Psychologists often speak of "cognitive traps" or "cognitive biases," referring to a wide range of common human responses to uncertainty. In this book I use the term "cognition trap" as a shorthand for rigid mental frameworks. I am focusing on those mind-sets that I as a historian see as most frequently undermining good judgment.

5. Jeffrey Goldberg, "A Little Learning," *New Yorker*, May 9, 2005.

Chapter 1: Exposure Anxiety

1. George Orwell, "Shooting an Elephant," www.online-literature .com/orwell/887. For an intriguing look at Orwell's writings through the lens of contemporary Burmese society, see Emma Larkin, *Finding George Orwell in Burma* (New York: Penguin, 2005).
2. Thucydides, *History of the Peloponnesian War* (New York: Penguin Books, 1986), 215–16.
3. Ibid., 217.
4. Ibid., 217–18.
5. Ibid., 219–21.
6. Scott Wilson, "Official Panel Accuses Israeli Leaders of Multiple Failures in Lebanon War," *Washington Post*, April 30, 2007.
7. Matthew McKay and Barbara Quick, *The Commitment Dialogues: How to Talk Your Way Through the Tough Times and Build a Stronger Relationship* (New York: McGraw-Hill, 2005), 67.
8. Ibid., 69.
9. Ibid., 69.
10. Conversation with the author, June 1, 2007.

Chapter 2: Causefusion

1. Charles Lamb, "A Dissertation Upon Roast Pig," in *The Complete Works and Letters of Charles Lamb* (New York: Random House, 1935), 108–11.
2. Michael Pollan, "Unhappy Meals," *New York Times*, January 28, 2007.
3. Pamela Spiro Wagner and Carolyn S. Spiro, *Divided Minds: Twin Sisters and Their Journey Through Schizophrenia* (New York: St. Martin's Press, 2005). Here is one of Wagner's disturbing accounts of her own paranoia. Sometimes the voices in her head tell her to slash her wrists. Much of the time she remains

convinced that she is trapped in a convoluted conspiracy, the purpose of which is never clear. When, for example, her regular dentist is unavailable to perform a routine filling, another dentist takes over. Pam believes that the dentist has implanted a microchip in her tooth, enabling the conspirators to keep her under constant surveillance. "The computers at the drugstore across the street, programmed by the five people, have tapped into my TV and monitor my activities with a special radar. If I go out, special agents keep every one of my movements under surveillance. A man lighting a cigarette near the drugstore uses his lighter to signal to another just down the street, warning him of my approach. Another alerts conspirators inside. Nothing I do, indoors or out, goes unremarked."

4. For more on studies of the disease see Mathijs Koopmans, "Double Bind Theory Revisited," 1997. www.goertzel.org/dynapsyc/1997/Koopmans.html.

5. Stephen Jay Gould, *The Mismeasure of Man* (New York: Norton, 1996).

6. Michael Yapko, "What Causes Depression?" *Psychology Today*, July 21, 2003.

7. For more on how psychiatric conditions have been diagnosed, see Alexander Spiegel, "The Dictionary of Disorder: How One Man Revolutionized Psychiatry," *New Yorker*, January 3, 2005.

8. David A. Karp, *Is It Me or My Meds? Living with Antidepressants* (Cambridge: Harvard University Press, 2006), 229. See also the works of Martin Seligman, especially *Learned Optimism: How to Change Your Mind and Your Life* (New York: Vintage Books, 2006).

9. Rob Slotow, Gus van Dyk, Joyce Poole, Bruce Page, and Andre Klocke, "Older Bull Elephants Control Young Males," *Nature*, November 23, 2000.

10. Elizabeth Gilbert, *Eat, Pray, Love: One Woman's Search for Everything Across Italy, India, and Indonesia* (New York: Penguin, 2007), 52.

11. For more on Sarno's theories and suggested treatment, see

John E. Sarno, MD, *The Divided Mind: The Epidemic of Mind-body Disorders* (New York: HarperCollins, 2006).

12. Hellinger has published many books in German with some English translations. For those interested in learning more, you might start with Bert Hellinger, *Was in Familien Krank Macht und Heilt: Ein Kurs fur Betroffene* (Heidelberg: Carl-Auer-Systeme, 2001).

13. For a thoughtful study of the documentary record, see Beth A. Fischer, *The Reagan Reversal: Foreign Policy and the End of the Cold War* (Columbia, MO: University of Missouri Press, 1997).

14. For information specifically on the prewar arms race, see David Stevenson, *Armaments and the Coming of War: Europe, 1904–1914* (Oxford: Clarendon, 1996). Stevenson writes that the arms races certainly hindered diplomacy, "yet armaments were the wheels and pistons of the locomotive of history, not the steam, and if considered in isolation they offer neither a sufficient nor an all-embracing explanation of the destruction of the peace" (421).

15. Allan Horowitz and Jerome Wakefield, *The Loss of Sadness: How Psychiatry Transformed Normal Sadness into Depressive Disorder* (New York: Oxford University Press, 2007), 165.

16. Ibid., 177.

Chapter 3: Flatview

1. For an accessible account of America's overthrow of Mossadegh, see Stephen Kinzer, *All the Shah's Men: An American Coup and the Roots of Middle East Terror* (Hoboken, NJ: John Wiley and Sons, 2003).

2. According to the 9/11 Commission, Iran lent aid and comfort to some of the hijackers who murdered three thousand people in New York, Washington, and on the plane that crashed in Pennsylvania.

3. Melanie Billings-Yun, *Decision Against War: Eisenhower and Dien Bien Phu, 1954* (New York: Columbia University Press, 1998), 1.

4. Robert S. McNamara, *In Retrospect: The Tragedy and Lessons of Vietnam* (New York: Vintage, 1996). McNamara's explanation of his actions—that he and the president saw Vietnam as part of the Cold War struggle—has not gone unchallenged. One scholar of the period, H. R. MacMaster, argues vigorously that Defense Secretary McNamara's claims about Washington's worldview are fictitious. The author charges that the defense secretary manipulated the information flow to President Johnson for political reasons. MacMaster insists that McNamara wanted to win the war with his theory of incremental escalation, thereby hamstringing the military from fighting the war with overwhelming force. See *Dereliction of Duty: Lyndon Johnson, Robert McNamara, the Joint Chiefs of Staff, and the Lies That Led to Vietnam* (New York: HarperPerennial, 1998).

5. Gurney to Creech Jones, December 19, 1948. See Christopher Bayly and Tim Harper, *Forgotten Wars: Freedom and Revolution in Southeast Asia* (Cambridge: Harvard University Press, 2007), 455.

6. John Nagl, *Counter-Insurgency Lessons from Malaya and Vietnam: Learning to Eat Soup with a Knife* (New York: Praeger, 2002), 87.

7. Chin Peng, as told to Ian Ward and Norma Miraflor, in *My Side of History: Recollections of the Guerrilla Leader Who Waged a Twelve-Year Anti-Colonial War Against British and Commonwealth Forces in the Jungles of Malaya* (Singapore: Media Masters, 2003).

8. Kumar Ramakrishna, *Emergency Propaganda: The Winning of Malayan Hearts and Minds, 1948–1958* (Richmond, UK: Curzon Press, 2002), 205–6.

9. For more on British and American army organizational learning, see Nagl, *Counter-Insurgency Lessons.*

10. McNamara, *In Retrospect.*

11. Ibid.

12. Jeffrey Goldberg, "A Little Learning," *New Yorker*, May 9, 2005. Italics added.

13. Dan Kindlon and Michael Thompson *Raising Cain: Protecting the Emotional Life of Boys* (New York: Ballantine Books, 1999).

Chapter 4: Cure-allism

1. Peter Reddaway, "Tainted Transactions: An Exchange (Response to Janine Wedel)," *National Interest*, Spring 2000.
2. Ibid., 98.
3. Jeffrey Sachs, "Perspective on Russia," *Los Angeles Times*, November 22, 1998.
4. Jeffrey Sachs, "Life After Communism," *Wall Street Journal*, November 17, 1999. Others have argued that Poland weathered the transition better than other Eastern European nations because it used shock therapy only briefly, then implemented a gradual process of privatization while building up the legal institutions necessary for a functioning and regulated capitalist economy.
5. The East Asian Tigers included Hong Kong, Singapore, South Korea, and Taiwan. The Southeast Asian Tigers included Indonesia, Malaysia, Thailand, and the Philippines.
6. Joseph Stiglitz, "What I Learned at the World Economic Crisis," *New Republic*, April 17, 2000.
7. The quotes and much of the explanation for the crisis in this section are drawn from Stiglitz, "What I Learned," as well as Stiglitz, *Globalization and Its Discontents* (New York: W. W. Norton, 2002). Although Stiglitz may be the most accessible writer on the crisis, for more scholarly explanations see David C. Kang, "Bad Loans to Good Friends: Money Politics and the Developmental State in South Korea," *International Organization* 56:2 (2002), 177–207; Gregory Noble, *The Asian Financial Crisis and the Architecture of Global Finance* (Cambridge: Cambridge University Press, 2000); Frederick D. Robins, "Asia's 1997 Crash: Its Character, Causes and Consequences," in *The East Asian Development Model: Economic Growth, Institutional Failure, and the Aftermath of Crisis*, ed. Frank-Juergen Richter (London: Macmillan, 2000); Lawrence H. Summers, "International Financial Crises: Causes, Prevention, and Cures," *American Economic Review* 90:2 (2000), 1–16. Naturally, there are books as critical of the World Bank as Stiglitz is of the IMF. See, for example, Bruce Rich, *Mortgaging the Earth: The World*

Bank, Environmental Impoverishment, and the Crisis of Development (Boston: Beacon Press,1994), 103–4. Rich writes of World Bank employees, "In their sealed offices in Washington, or in their short stays in five-star hotels in tropical capitals, many staff and the executive directors were so removed from the consequences of their actions that they acted as if they were dealing with a make-believe world on another planet than the one they inhabited, one that could be put back together again after their mistakes." See also the equally ideological works Kevin Danaher, ed., *50 Years Is Enough: The Case Against the World Bank and the International Monetary Fund* (Boston: South End, 1994), and Graham Hancock, *Lords of Poverty: The Free-Wheeling Lifestyles, Power, Prestige and Corruption of the Multi-Billion-Dollar Aid Business* (London: Macmillan, 1989).

8. Joseph Stiglitz, "Financial Hypocrisy," *Economist's View*, November 20, 2007, economistsview.typepad.com/economists view/2007/11/joseph-stiglitz.html, accessed March 14, 2008.

9. For a brief overview of private prisons see Judith Greene, "Prison Privatization: Recent Developments in the United States," paper presented at the International Conference on Penal Abolition, May 12, 2000. A more detailed study is Joel Dyer, *The Perpetual Prisoner Machine: How America Profits from Crime* (Boulder: Westview Press, 2000).

10. Ernst Ulrich von Weizsäcker, ed., *Limits to Privatization* (London: Earthscan, 2005), 17–40. For more on Bolivia's water crisis, see William Finnegan, "Leasing the Rain: The World Is Running Out of Fresh Water, and the Fight to Control It Has Begun," *New Yorker*, April 8, 2002, 43; and Jim Shultz, "The Politics of Water in Bolivia," *Nation*, January 28, 2005.

11. James C. Scott, *Seeing Like a State: How Certain Schemes to Improve the Human Condition Have Failed* (New Haven: Yale University Press, 1998), 343–46.

Chapter 5: Infomania

1. Joint Center for Operations Analysis, Joint Forces Command, *Iraq Perspectives Project*, 64 (www.jfcom.mil/newslink/story archive/2006/ipp.pdf).
2. Seiichi Iwao, *Biographical Dictionary of Japanese History* (New York: Kodansha America, 1978) 411–12.
3. Yosuke Matsuoka, *Building Up Manchuria* (Tokyo: The Toppan Printing Company, 1938), 2.
4. Ibid., 6.
5. William L. Langer and S. Everett Gleason, *The Undeclared War, 1940–1941* (Gloucester, MA: P. Smith, 1968), 28.
6. *The Magic Documents: Summaries and Transcripts of the Top Secret Diplomatic Communications of Japan, 1938–1945*, ed. Paul Kesaris (Washington, D.C.: University Publications of America, 1980), #1887, H11161, Matsuoka in Tokyo to Washington, September 2, 1940. "Magic" was the code name for America's code-breaking operation against Japanese military and diplomatic transmissions. If we compare those secret, decoded cables with the records of what Matsuoka and Tojo were saying in cabinet conferences, we can see further evidence of how determined these men were to ally with Nazi Germany.
7. Ike Nobutaka, ed., *Japan's Decision for War: Records of the 1941 Policy Conferences* (Stanford, CA: Stanford University Press, 1967), 100.
8. Ibid., 101.
9. Ibid.
10. Ibid., 104.
11. Joseph C. Grew, *Ten Years in Japan* (New York: Simon & Schuster, 1944), 481.
12. Diego de Landa, *Yucatán Before and After the Conquest* (New York: Dover, 1978), 82. Three books and fragments of a fourth survived destruction. Only later, back in Spain, did de Landa translate them. These codices remain the only known written records of the Mayan language.
13. Mark W. McLeod, *The Vietnamese Response to French Intervention, 1862–1874* (New York: Praeger, 1991), 19.

14. When Gia Long subsequently told his court that the former rulers had no dealings with the Europeans, he was either exaggerating or he did not know his own history. From as early as the mid-1500s Vietnamese began recovering European cannons and weapons from Dutch, Spanish, and Portuguese shipwrecks. They then hired European craftsmen, mostly Englishmen, to build foundries for them. The Vietnamese became so skilled at the art that in 1678 they requested an English gun founder to visit, not to teach them how to build foundries, but so the Vietnamese could observe the latest European techniques. In one case, they ordered twenty cannons from England but rejected seven of them because they did not meet the high standards of the Vietnamese. See Nicholas Tarlang, ed., *The Cambridge History of Southeast Asia*, vol. 1 (Cambridge: Cambridge University Press, 1992).

15. John Crawfurd, *Journal of an Embassy from the Governor-General of India to the Courts of Siam and Cochin China: Exhibiting a View of the Actual State of Those Kingdoms* (London: Henry Colburn, 1828; Oxford: Oxford University Press, 1967). Citations are to the Oxford edition. See diary entry for September 28, 1828.

16. The same problems in manufacturing dogged the civil administration. The Vietnamese bureaucracy had been trained for generations in the Chinese Confucian classics. Those classics included philosophy, history, and poetry—all extremely useful fields for stretching the mind and developing well-rounded scholars, but less practical for learning the intricacies of international trade. Confucian training made it harder for Vietnamese officials to adapt to a changing world where greater technical knowledge was essential.

17. McLeod, *Vietnamese Response*, 291.

18. One of the leading scholars of Siamese history has argued that the openness of elites to new ideas can be traced back to Rama I, who took power in 1782. According to this view, the monarchy became more responsive to and communicative with its subjects because its elites were profoundly affected by the inadequate rulers who preceeded them in the 1770s.

Rama I's immediate predecessor reigned during a destructive war with the Burmese, ending in Siamese defeat. Thus, the reforms of King Mongkut (Rama IV), Wyatt suggests, are the legacy of Rama I's reforms, forged from necessity. See David K. Wyatt, "The 'Subtle Revolution' of King Rama I," in Alexander Woodside, ed., *Moral Order and the Question of Change* (New Haven: Yale University Southeast Asian Studies, 1982), 9–52.

19. Sir John Bowring, *The Kingdom and People of Siam* (London: John W. Parker and Son, 1857; Oxford: Oxford University Press, 1969), vol. II, 279. Citations are to the Oxford edition.

20. Ibid., 307.

21. For more on Mongkut's and Chulalongkorn's reigns, see David K. Wyatt, *Thailand: A Short History* (New Haven: Yale University Press, 1984).

22. Some historians have argued that it didn't matter that Siam avoided colonization because Siamese rulers instituted a process of "internal colonization," manufacturing a police-patrolled surveillance society, subjecting the Siamese people to colonial-like conditions under Siamese control. See Thongchai Winichakul, *Siam Mapped: A History of the Geo-Body of a Nation* (Honolulu: University of Hawaii Press, 1994). But even this provocative view does not explain how Siam escaped European conquest. Part of the answer, it seems to me, must be found in the leaders' relationship to information.

23. More on Jim Simons can be found in the following articles: Hal Lux, "The Secret World of Jim Simons," *Institutional Investor*, November 2000; Andrea Katz and Eleanor Lee, "The Alternative Rich List: Money Isn't Everything, Especially When You've Got Loads," *Financial Times*, September 23, 2006.

24. County of New York: IAS Part 27, New York County Clerk's Office, Supreme Court of the State of New York, Index No. 603839/03, Part No. 18575, filed April 2007.

Chapter 6: Mirror Imaging

1. Deborah Tannen, *You Just Don't Understand: Men and Women in Conversation* (New York: Ballantine Books, 1990).

2. John Gray, *Men Are from Mars, Women Are from Venus: The Classic Guide to Understanding the Opposite Sex* (New York: Quill, 2004).

3. For a compelling history of postwar Japan, see John W. Dower, *Embracing Defeat: Japan in the Wake of World War II* (New York: W. W. Norton, 1999). Many of the details in this section are drawn from chapter 4.

4. A chilling account of Soviet behavior toward East German women after the war can be found in Norman M. Naimark, *The Russians in Germany: A History of the Soviet Zone of Occupation, 1945–1949* (Cambridge, MA: Harvard University Press, 1995), ch. 2.

5. Bernard Fall, *Hell in a Very Small Place* (New York: Knopf, 1966), 54–56.

6. For years after the event, General Henri Navarre, the battle's mastermind, maintained that Dien Bien Phu was a necessary place to confront the enemy. By establishing a stronghold deep in the enemy's terrain, Navarre insisted, France could prevent a Vietminh thrust into Laos. The historian Douglas Porch has argued that Dien Bien Phu was in fact essential for control of the lucrative opium trade, which both France and the Vietminh relied upon to fund their armies. Without access to that opium, France believed it could not prevail. Denying France the drug trade therefore became a Vietminh prime objective. For more on how opium influenced the war, see Douglas Porch, *The French Secret Services: From the Dreyfus Affair to the Gulf War* (New York: Farrar, Straus and Giroux, 1995). For a detailed history of the Dien Bien Phu battle, see Martin Windrow, *The Last Valley: Dien Bien Phu and the French Defeat in Vietnam* (London: Weidenfeld & Nicolson, 2004).

7. Fall, *Hell*, 101.

8. Ibid., 452.

9. Melanie Billings-Yun, *Decision Against War: Eisenhower and Dien Bien Phu, 1954* (New York: Columbia University Press, 1998), 106.

10. Ibid., 151.

11. George C. Herring and Richard H. Immerman, "Eisenhower, Dulles, and Dienbienphu: 'The Day We Didn't Go to War' Revisited," *Journal of American History* 71, no. 2 (September 1984), 343–63.

12. Billings-Yun, *Decision*, 152.

13. Ibid., 150. This quote is a paraphrase by NSC head Robert Cutler.

14. Some of Hyder Akbar's audio journal can be heard online at www.thisamericanlife.org. See also Said Hyder Akbar and Susan Burton, *Come Back to Afghanistan: A California Teenager's Story* (New York: Bloomsbury, 2005).

15. Arthur M. Schlesinger Jr., *A Thousand Days: John F. Kennedy in the White House* (New York: Fawcett Premier, 1965), 748. Schlesinger is known to have at times embellished JFK's gifts. He offers no corroborating evidence of this claim regarding the reconnaissance of U.S. jets, but even if this particular anecdote is not entirely accurate, there is substantial evidence that Kennedy tried hard to see the crisis through Soviet eyes.

Chapter 7: Static Cling

1. Jason Sokol, *There Goes My Everything: White Southerners in the Age of Civil Rights, 1945–1975* (New York: Knopf, 2006), 185–86.

2. Thurmond had fathered a child with an African-American maid in 1925. The senator secretly supported his daughter financially well into her adult life. It is not yet known precisely how this relationship influenced his evolving views on race.

3. One weakness of this section is that the story of Gerstner's turnaround is based solely on Gerstner's telling. Unlike all other sections, for the IBM example I have found no corrobo-

rating evidence to support the CEO's many claims about what he did. However, the main point of this episode is in fact to show that business leaders can recognize static cling and work to overcome it. Assuming that Gerstner may have embellished his own contributions to the turnaround, the point about static cling nevertheless remains valid.

4. Rick Weiss and Justin Gillis, "Monsanto Beats Farmer in Patent Fight: Canadian Court Upholds Claim to Gene-Altered Seed," *Washington Post*, May 22, 2004.

5. Kelly Patterson, "Seeds of Discontent: A Blessing or a Curse to Mankind? Critics of Genetically Modified Food and Grain-Industry Giants Await UN Ruling on 'Suicide Seeds,'" *Ottawa Citizen*, March 5, 2006.

6. Edison's claim to have produced the earliest audio recordings fell into dispute in March 2008, when audio historians discovered a sound recording from 1860, produced on a phonautogram by the French inventor Édouard-Léon Scott de Martinville. Scott's first recording came seventeen years before Edison invented the phonograph. See Jody Rosen, "Researchers Play Tune Recorded Before Edison," *New York Times*, March 27, 2008.

Chapter 8: Cognition-Trapped in Iraq

1. See Yossef Bodansky, *Bin Laden: The Man Who Declared War on America* (Rocklin, CA: Forum, 2001).

2. National Commission on Terrorist Attacks, *The 9/11 Commission Report: The Final Report of the National Commission on Terrorist Attacks upon the United States* (New York: W. W. Norton, 2004).

3. Philip Tetlock, a sociologist at the University of California, Berkeley, has argued that experts are more often correct in their judgment when they have a broad knowledge ranging across many fields. Specialists with a deep knowledge of only one field, Tetlock claims, make less accurate predictions. But even those with a broad knowledge base still sometimes commit

blunders. I think the problem of cognition traps helps to explain why. See Philip Tetlock, *Expert Political Judgment: How Good Is It? How Can We Know?* (Princeton, NJ: Princeton University Press, 2005).

4. See Rajiv Chandrasekaran, *Imperial Life in the Emerald City: Inside Iraq's Green Zone* (New York: Knopf, 2006). Chandrasekaran's account, like any journalist's writings, must be read with the understanding that some degree of sensationalizing is likely present. Life inside the Green Zone, as he depicts it, seems colonial in its grandeur, especially juxtaposed to Baghdad city life outside it. Naturally, any administrative center required independent electricity for phones, computers, and light, not just air conditioning and other comforts, and the Green Zone provided this.

5. Michael R. Gordon and General Bernard E. Trainor, *Cobra II: The Inside Story of the Invasion and Occupation of Iraq* (New York: Random House, 2006), 148.

6. *Frontline*, July 17, 2003. "Truth, War and Consequences: Interviews: General Jay Garner," PBS, www.pbs.org/wgbh/pages/frontline/shows/truth/interviews/garner.html, accessed June 17, 2005.

7. Bradley Graham and Thomas E. Ricks, "Pentagon Blamed for Lack of Postwar Planning in Iraq," *Washington Post*, April 1, 2005.

8. Tucker Carlson, *Crossfire*, April 1, 2004.

9. The aid worker asked not to be identified because his comments to me were not vetted by his organization.

10. A graphic and intricately detailed depiction of this battle has been provided in Bing West, *No True Glory: A Frontline Account of the Battle for Fallujah* (New York: Bantam Books, 2005).

11. Bruce R. Pirnie and Edward O'Connell, *Counterinsurgency in Iraq, 2003–2006, RAND Counterinsurgency Study*, vol. 2 (Santa Monica, CA: The RAND Corporation, 2008).

Chapter 9: Working Toward Wisdom

1. Mike May's story has been chronicled in Robert Kurson, *Crashing Through: A True Story of Risk, Adventure, and the Man Who Dared to See* (New York: Random House, 2007).

INDEX

A NOTE ON THE AUTHOR

Zachary Shore is associate professor of national security affairs at the Naval Postgraduate School and a senior fellow at the Institute of European Studies at the University of California, Berkeley. He has served on the policy planning staff at the U.S. Department of State and at the Council on Foreign Relations. He has also worked as a national security fellow at Harvard's Olin Institute for Strategic Studies. Shore earned his doctorate from Oxford and has won numerous academic honors, including Harvard's Derek Bok Teaching Award. He is the author of *What Hitler Knew* and *Breeding Bin Ladens* and lives in Berkeley, California.